Real Estate Lifestyle™, Live the Real Estate Lifestyle™ and America's Real Estate Cashflow Expert™ are trademarks of:
Real Estate Lifestyle, LLC
680 Louis Drive
Warminster, PA 18974 USA

Your FREE Gifts and Bonuses are available at
www.livetherealestatelifestyle.com

"This publication is designed to provide accurate and authoritative information in regard to the subject matter covered. It is sold with the understanding that the publisher is not engaged in rendering legal, accounting, or other professional service. If legal or other expert assistance is required, the services of a competent professional person should be sought."

—From a declaration of principles jointly adopted by a committee of the American Bar Association and a committee of the Publishers Association

Canale, James A.
Canale, Jim
Live the Real Estate Lifestyle: Seven Simple Steps You Can Take Today To Leave the Rat Race and Start Living the Life You've Always Wanted!
p. cm.
ISBN 0-1234567-1-2 Pbk.
1. Personal Finance.
2. Business Education.
3. Success – Financial.
4. Investments. I. Title

Printed in the United States of America

LIVE THE REAL ESTATE LIFESTYLE

Seven Steps That You Can Take To Leave The 'Rat Race' And Start Living The Life style You've Always Wanted

JIM CANALE

authorHOUSE®

AuthorHouse™
1663 Liberty Drive, Suite 200
Bloomington, IN 47403
www.authorhouse.com
Phone: 1-800-839-8640

First published by AuthorHouse

ISBN: 9-7814-3435-8707

First published by AuthorHouse 6/17/2008

Printed in the United States of America
Bloomington, Indiana

LIVE THE REAL
ESTATE LIFESTYLE

**Seven Steps You Can Take Today
To Leave the Rat Race
And Start Living the Lifestyle
You've Always Wanted!**

Jim Canale

What Other Successful People Are Saying About

Live the Real Estate Lifestyle

"Jim Canale understands the core of what it takes to become successful in the money game. And his timing for you could not be better. It's one thing to think you know…*yet quite another to actually pull the trigger and be in the game.* Jim's simple, direct, in-your-face process will get you into the game and onto your dreams today.

He understands that it's not finding or executing the deal that is hard, it's the war between your own ears that makes it tough. He knows how to get you to win that battle and succeed!

He is not only a great Real Estate investor, but a great educator, motivator and a voracious student himself…which at the end of the day is one of the things that makes him great…and what will make you win."

> **Blair Singer**, Rich Dad Advisor, Facilitator, Trainer
> Author of the books *SalesDogs, The ABC's of Building a Business Team that Wins*, and the soon to be released, *Little Voice Mastery*
> **www.salesdogs.com**

"Jim has taught thousands of people how to understand and successfully apply the exact same principles taught in this book to reduce fear and get started in Real Estate. I recommend Jim's book wholeheartedly!"

> **Kendra Todd**, Host of HGTV's *My House is Worth What?*
> Best-selling author of *Risk & Grow Rich*, Winner of *The Apprentice 3*
> **www.kendratodd.com**

"As a best-selling author and an international speaker, I meet thousands of people every year who ask me how to get started on the path to financial freedom. Well, THIS book is a great place to start! Whether you think Real Estate is for you or not, Jim shows you how to use proven success strategies to get everything that you want!"

> **T. Harv Eker,** Author of the New York Times #1 Best Seller,
> *Secrets of the Millionaire Mind*
> **www.tharveker.com**

Even More Praise For

Live the Real Estate Lifestyle

"There are usually four things that will stop a Real Estate investor cold in their tracks—Fear of Financial Loss, Fear of Failure, Fear of Making a Mistake, and Fear of Obligation. Jim Canale has a unique way of obliterating those Fears. He teaches you the *'experiential learning secrets'* that will make you successful in days—instead of having to wait for what usually takes decades to learn."

Terry Wygal
Author of *7 Fatal Mistakes Every Real Estate Investor Makes*
www.TotalFinancialLiberty.com

"I don't care whether you're an *Average Joe* that's brand new to Real Estate, or if you've been a savvy investor for years—*Live the Real Estate Lifestyle* offers ANY man or woman, valuable hard-nosed business wisdom from someone who really has *been there and done that.* I consult with LOADS of supposed Real Estate *gurus* who, when you pull the curtain back, are nothing more than one-trick ponies living week to week. What Jim Canale shares in this book, is a genuine, eye-opening, quick-start education that benefits those looking to profit not only in Real Estate, but in business, and in life, as well. Information like this is worth a small fortune for those folks who have the gumption—*and the balls*—to really live out their dreams and truly start enjoying *The Real Estate Lifestyle.*"

Craig Garber, Author of the book *Seductive Selling*
America's Top Direct-Response Copywriter
www.KingOfCopy.com

"Jim Canale IS America's Real Estate Cashflow Expert. No one else explains so clearly how an ordinary working person can start to build wealth. Jim's method of building wealth through cashflow Real Estate is simple: find an asset to cover the car payment, find an asset to pay for your home. This is the true method of building wealth and Jim's book shows you how."

Dwight Miller
www.BlackGeniusNetwork.com

"When I first met Jim five years ago, I had just become a Realtor. I had invested in Real Estate before and I had acquired a fair amount of property. Though working with Jim as his Realtor®, I discovered that he doesn't do things the way *normal* people do. He is different! He does things in contrast to what everyone else does, and he's achieved a whole lot of success that way. Believe me, I personally saw those checks coming in at his settlements and I wanted that for myself. I'm a big believer in Living Free, yet I wasn't living that way at the time and Jim was, so, I asked him to Coach me in this way of life."

"Over the next few years with Jim I discovered how a business operates, how money is managed, how time is best utilized, and how life can best be prioritized. As a result, my wallet grew — into the millions! My own Real Estate investing business has grown incredibly, and as a result of Jim's teachings, I don't have to spend more than a dozen hours a week on it! I am now able to create money at will, I have multiple streams of recurring income, and I get to enjoy spending more time with my family and friends...vacationing — three so far this year — going to the park with my children, whatever I want!"

"But most incredibly, I don't have to stress out at night wondering where my life has gone and how am I going to find the money to buy it back. I dedicate my time to personal and interpersonal self-betterment. This is what I've discovered by working with Jim. The man has changed my life and he'll change yours, too!"

Joe Hurst
Real Estate Investor
CheapAssRealEstate.com

"Before I met Jim Canale, I had been investing in Real Estate since 2003. I was purchasing a few properties here and there and not making much headway into the grand lifestyle promised by the promoters of many Real Estate success courses."

"In 2006, I met Jim Canale. The first lesson I learned from Jim — *never stop learning.* Jim's friendship and guidance over just the past year has caused me to do some strange things... *Quit my job, start a business, and invest in Real Estate like a professional does!* This complete and incredible change in lifestyle and thinking I credit entirely to Jim Canale.

I live the life I choose to live, using Jim's advice and guidance."

"If you want to live the lifestyle and have the income you want and deserve, read Jim's book and follow his advice. I did, and look what happened: _I am happy, wealthy, and in complete control of my life._ Thanks, Jim!"

Dan Tuey
North America's Fear Removal Expert
Enlightened Bad Asses
www.enlightenedbadasses.com

"I met Jim Canale as an experienced Real Estate investor, however, I know now that I was going about it all wrong. I was doing everything myself: attempting to save money and I was losing valuable time that could have been used for golf, karate, family time and other activities. It literally took six months on the "Do It Yourself Train" to complete what would have taken a professional contractor two weeks. Using Jim's system I've been able to put myself in the true business I wanted to be in The Real Estate Lifestyle Business. I am now able to schedule my own time and spend it doing the important things in my life."

"I have to tell you in my very first deal after discovering Jim's system, I was able to purchase a property that gives me positive cashflow of $1,000.00 a month and I received $40,000.00 tax-free cash back at closing. Jim's system is simple and fool-proof. Anybody can do it! After one year of using this system I was able to tell my boss "I'm losing money coming to work!" I know I would not have the 2 Million Dollar Real Estate investment business I have today if Jim had not shared his business experience and insight. And now I'm able to share this system with my own family and friends."

Victor Milbourne
VCT Investments
www.juststartingrealestateinvestor.com

"Since meeting Jim Canale two years ago I have made close to $200,000 in Real Estate using his methods. I do it setting aside only one day each week—Thursday. In addition, Jim's business guidance has helped my Investment Management business double in assets that we manage—from $50 million to $100 million and I've experienced a 40% reduction in the time that I spend in that business. My wife and I have been able to pay off our home loan of $150,000, and greatly increase our lifestyle."

"Most importantly, since we cannot bear children, we can now afford the $40,000 to go through the adoption process without worrying about how it will get paid for! I am proud to have Jim as a Coach and close personal friend. You hold in your hands a rare and unique opportunity to learn from the best! You need to read this book and then put Jim's principles into action!"

Patrick Clark
Investment Manager and Real Estate Investor

www.corestates.us

Free Reader Bonus!

Now, claim your TWO FREE BONUS GIFTS
worth over $179 just for buying this book!

Congratulations on your investment in yourself! As my way of saying "Thank You" for letting me play an active part in your journey to financial freedom, I've prepared two exclusive Free Implementation and Action Gifts for you. These two tools are worth $179 and will help jump-start your action plan for Real Estate success. They're both yours free as a reader—and implementer—of *Live the Real Estate Lifestyle.*

All you have to do to get your two bonus Implementation and Action gifts is visit my special website at **www.livetherealestatelifestyle.com/Resources** and they are yours free! Thank you and enjoy the book!

This book is dedicated to my wonderful children, Julie, Sammie, and Jimmy. May you live your lives with passion, and enjoy lifelong financial freedom and personal independence.

This book is also dedicated to all the people who know there's more to life than getting up and going to work each day. You're not crazy…there IS much more and you deserve to have it all! I sincerely hope that this book helps you get started along your way.

Acknowledgements

Many thanks to Joe Hurst, my friend, my business partner and my Real Estate agent. You keep delivering the goods, no matter what the market conditions or political situations are. Every business partner should strive to be like you!

A warm and fond thank you to the many listeners of my Live The Real Estate Lifestyle Radio programs, my students and my members who have allowed me to share in your successes, your trials in getting started, and your celebrations after conquering your fear and achieving your dreams. You are all to be admired. I wish you continued success.

I'd also like to thank my own Mentors and Coaches through the years—Robert and Kim Kiyosaki, Dan Kennedy, Bill Glazer, Ron LeGrand, T. Harv Eker, Bill Brooks, Blair Singer, Anthony Robbins, Jay Abraham, Dwight Miller and Bruce Morrow. Much of my success and many millions of dollars are a direct result of your influence.

Getting a book to the finish line takes a lot of hard work by many talented people. I'd like to thank my publisher Author-House, Tam Thompson for her creative support, Marilyn Lois Polak for her editing skills, my Graphics and Tech guy Dusan Simovic, 1106 for the cover design, and Danyhel McClea for exceeding my expectations on a daily basis!

Finally, my gratitude to you, dear reader. It's my sincerest wish that this book launches your journey to financial freedom and independence, using Real Estate and cash flow principles. Here's to <u>YOUR</u> ultimate Real Estate Lifestyle!

Contents

The Author's Warning!

BEWARE!

Reading this book and FULLY participating in its exercises can positively and TOTALLY change your life…

FOREVER!

What's This "Real Estate Lifestyle" Thing All About, Anyway?

Today is my 38th birthday. I'm celebrating it in a way some people might find unusual. Some of you may even believe it's impossible for you. However, I'm living proof it's not impossible. In fact, it's even easier to have the life I have — *and you can get* — than it is to go to work every day and do what most people do.

Right now, I'm sitting next to a crystal clear turquoise ocean. I'm on a small collection of islands in the eastern Caribbean called the Turks and Caicos Islands. I'll be here for the next three weeks.

Now, I know there's not much special about taking three weeks 'off' to hang out on an island, staying in the Presidential Suite with 24-hour Butler service, private chefs, wait-staff to bring pool side cocktails, personal nanny service for the children, daily scuba diving in the number two rated dive spot in the entire world, and the best Cuban cigars and coffee from around the world. There's nothing that special about staying at the TOP-rated family resort in the entire world, having access to world-class cuisine, partying in one of seven hot tubs, swim-up bars, parasailing, horseback riding, not to mention unbelievable sunsets! I'm well aware anyone who can write a $55,000 check could be doing exactly what I'm doing now. **However, my family and I are here for FREE!**

You see, I pay for everything with Real Estate money — money I make by being a decider, not a laborer or an employee. It takes a long time as an employee to save up $55,000 to "blow" on a vacation. But in this case, it took me less than eight total hours of my personal involvement to get the money together for this three week vacation. The deal I used to pay for this vacation netted me over $75,000. So I still have another $20,000 left over to play with when I get home!

If you take $75,000 and divide it by the eight hours of my personal involvement, I was paid $9,375 per hour for my time. If you're making that kind of money now, there's no reason to continue reading this book. You've already got a winning formula and you should stick to it. As they say, *"If it ain't broke, don't fix it!"* But if you're not making that kind of money to spend *any way that you choose*, then this book is for you.

Big Idea #1: REAL ESTATE IS A LIFESTYLE BUSINESS

That statement is much, *much* bigger than it appears on the surface. Real Estate is NOT about the bricks and sticks. It's about two things, really.

First, it's about the lifestyle Real Estate affords you. Let me offer a few more examples. My wife and I wanted a new pool in the back yard. It cost us $60,000 plus landscaping. Most people buy a pool by making a deposit and then paying off the balance with on time monthly payments with interest for three to five years. I simply wrote a check. I got the money by selling a house to a first-time home buyer. My time involved about five hours. We wanted to go to the Caribbean last year — no problem; just two wholesale fees and we were on our way!

Last year, I wanted the new Jaguar XK8 convertible for only $2,000 per month on a two-year lease. So I bought a 10-unit apartment building that throws off $2,000 per month in profits! The good news is when I'm sick of the car, I get to keep the asset that pays for the car. And I'll buy a new building to pay for my next new car lease.

I wear great clothes...Armani, Robert Graham, Indigo Palms. Great shoes...Barker Black, and Prada. I love a great watch, too...Rolex, Cartier...And on and on. Whatever it is that I want, I equate it to a Real Estate transaction. My solid gold and diamond Presidential Rolex cost me about $60,000.

For me it was two rental houses and a contract assignment. I decided I wanted the watch at the Bellagio in Las Vegas in the beginning of November. I had the watch in time for Thanksgiving.

The second reason **Real Estate Is a Lifestyle Business** is this: Real Estate does not have to be a full-time venture. You don't have to unclog toilets; you don't have to be a Contractor; and you don't need to spend all your weekends doing it! Real Estate, done right, is NOT a do-it-yourself business. In Real Estate, fifth-grade math reigns supreme, C-students thrive, and folks with ADD finally stand a chance! Real Estate is about getting the experts to BE experts while you make informed decisions and reap the rewards. Don't worry if you don't really get the concept yet. By the end of the first chapter this will all make sense.

So tell me. Would you like to know how I do it? How I made enough money to pay for this Caribbean vacation in just three months, using none of my own money? How I spent just eight hours of *my own time* to get it done? Of course you would, and I'm not just going to tell you how I did it, I'm also going to give you a **Tactical Action and Implementation Plan** you can use immediately, so you can do it, too. Would you like that? I thought you would!

You Don't Have To Be Donald Trump!

To get the things I want in life, I hand pick lucrative Real Estate deals that could be done by just about anyone. However, most people think deals like these are out of their reach. They think they have to have hundreds of thousands of dollars in the bank, or great credit, or years of specialized education. Well, you don't need to be Donald Trump to get these results!

Let me be frank: people like Donald Trump are very rare.

He's rare because he has more than a billion dollars. Think about that: $1,000,000,000. That's one heck of a lot of zeroes. The truth is, 99.9% of all Real Estate investors don't make anywhere near a billion dollars. Not ever.

But you know what? Plenty of regular, ordinary people just like you and me make Real Estate work! Hey, I'm a just a regular guy who came up the hard way, too. Lots of us are making millions of dollars in Real Estate, right now. Would you be satisfied to make several million instead of shooting for a billion? *I know I am!*

Picture this: Three years from now, you've made your million dollars in Real Estate. You're living in a big house with a big swimming pool out back, a sports car and a Harley in the garage. You don't have to work—you live off of your investments, which put a nice, big, fat check in your mailbox every month. You take two or three vacations anywhere in the world every year and you have a fabulous spouse and children who adore you. What more could you want?

To become a billionaire takes a ton of hard work every single day. Trump works 18 hours a day! They say he starts his days at 5 AM and goes straight through till 5 PM. Then he heads out for a business dinner and networking events to make more connections! His head hits the pillow by 11 PM, so he can do it all over again the next day. To be a billionaire also takes a whole lot of luck. You have to be incredibly smart and shrewd. Sure, Donald Trump came from a comfortable background, but he's still worked his tail off, even to the point of ruining marriages.

That's not what I mean when I say the phrase, *Lifestyle Business.* A Lifestyle Business is about autonomy—being able to do it when you want to do it, NOT about you doing all the work. It's about you making decisions based on good verifiable information other people—your business team—provides you. Anybody can do that. This book shows you how.

Being a millionaire is now something anyone can do—even you! **Especially** you. Because you're who this book is for. The people who have made millions with Real Estate are too many to count. Heck, the people I meet in my Real Estate Lifestyle workshops and trainings are regular people just like you—not upper-class people whose Daddy or Mommy gave them a few million dollars and said, "Go invest in Real Estate and make something of yourself." That's not hard to do.

My Real Estate Lifestyle System is designed for people who haven't had everything handed to them. People who have had to work for what they have. People whose family lives may not be perfect. People who don't necessarily look like movie stars. People who have had some tough breaks. Regular people who do the daily grind. People sick of working their butts off to make their bosses rich! All these people become successful once they decide they're ready for a change.

No looking back! Now's the time for change. Are you ready to join them? If you are, it's time to get started! Let me show you how. Now, onward!

Jim Canale

July 20, 2007

Providenciales, Turks and Caicos Islands

Chapter 1: Learning Habits

The Two Reasons Most
People Don't Succeed

Learning Habits—The Two Reasons
Most People Don't Succeed

This chapter is a critical MUST READ for those who really want to succeed at *anything!* For more years than I care to count, I've been watching people needlessly struggle to get started in Real Estate investing. Over the next few pages I'll explain exactly WHY people struggle, and exactly why YOU don't need to struggle anymore. We all know people who make lots of money in Real Estate, and that's the instant attraction of Real Estate as an investment vehicle. Unfortunately that very factor also makes the late-night infomercial guru pitch so convincing for "Get Rich Quick" schemes in Real Estate products. Believe me, I know. I own just about all them. If I sold all the Real Estate books and tapes and boot camps I've bought and unloaded them on eBay, I'd soon have enough money to buy another rental property — outright — in cash!

In one of those "instant results" Real Estate products I purchased, a national infomercial guru stated on his motivational video that his years of results proved people were twice as likely to buy his course a second time, than they were to actually buy an investment property! When I saw him "look me in the eye" and tell me that, it really got me thinking. Mostly because I knew he was right! For me, it was my third time buying his course. I bought the blue version, the green version and the black version. I freely admit it! And I feel no shame.

Lots of other people are repeat buyers of such products, too.

And here's why. There was something I kept looking for — but just couldn't find. I was following his instructions... Bringing donuts to the nice ladies at the courthouse, reading carefully through the deed and mortgage record books, subscribing to certain law publications, going to property auctions, driving through certain neighborhoods… I was doing everything I was told — yet I got no tangible result. Sure, I had grown in my *theoretical knowledge,* but the only real results to measure are in the form of CASH — that's what allows me to live the lifestyle I desire. Can you relate?

The truth is, none of those books or tapes got me where I am today. Maybe they even delayed my ability to make a decision to *actually take action and buy my first property.* Now, I'm not trying to say books and tapes are bad — especially since I've just written the one you're reading — but what I am saying is this: like most people, *I made the big mistake of thinking I needed to know EVERY SINGLE THING about Real Estate before actually making my first offer.* Knowing exactly how the foreclosure process works, or how a short sale works, or how to install new windows, will not help you overcome the reason you don't have any property now. That information could even hinder your ability to actually get a deal done!

Each time I embarked on another one of those books or study series, I actually felt like I was doing something to accomplish my goal of becoming a very Rich Real Estate investor. Back then, I did not realize:

**LEARNING IS NOT A
SUBSTITUTE FOR ACTION!**

The Number One Reason Why People "Fail"

Continuous learning without doing gave me the justification I needed to not be embarrassed by my **FEAR**. And that, my friend, is problem number one. Did you get that? Fear is the leading reason we don't do things we know will be good for us. Please don't feel badly. You're not to blame here. There's a very specific reason fear's stopping you from getting what you most want in life!

Humans are what's called "experiential learners." Can you still do calculus today? If you didn't ever learn calculus, can you still do trigonometry, or algebra? How about geometry? About 95% of the people I meet say they cannot—even those with college degrees. One person I asked is a Professor of Mathematics at a prestigious local university in Philadelphia. He can still do trigonometry, but not calculus, which he says makes his head hurt! Typically, most of us can't do it, and not because we're stupid. Blame the faulty method used to learn the subject matter—*rote memorization.*

Here's a second example explaining experiential learning and why it works. Can you still ride a bike? Of course! But let's advance this concept a little further—can you ride ANY bike? I could put *any* bicycle in any parking lot, anywhere in the world, and you would be able to ride it. Magic? Not really. There's a simple explanation for this "miracle."

Remember how you learned to ride a bike? Picture the day in your mind's eye for a minute. You got on the bike, and Mom or Dad held the back of the seat for you. They told you to pedal and as you did they ran behind you—still holding the back of the bike—and when they felt you were balanced enough they let go of the back of the bike and you pedaled along. And then it happened! Suddenly you looked back and saw that no one was holding you up any more. In that split second the handle bars began to wobble and shake, you lost your balance and fell over. Sure it hurt, but Mom or Dad came running up to you, kissed the boo-boo on your knee, and put you right back on the bike. Just a few more tries—doing the exact same thing—and you were finally able to ride the bike!

After a few more days of experience, it was second nature, wasn't it? It no longer mattered whether you were on your bike, or on a friends' bike, you could now ride. The **fear** of losing your balance and falling off was gone! If you were like me, you were probably riding with no hands just a short time later.

Human beings naturally learn through this experiential process. It's instinctual for us. Have you ever watched a baby learn how to walk? They crawl, then they pull themselves up, then they fall, then they lean on a coffee table, then they let go, then they fall, then they do it again and again, until they learn. In fact, we all learned how to walk the exact same way.

This experiential process is truly our natural human learning system, and we use it to learn everything. That is, until we get to school. There, we encounter a different way of learning. Most of us struggle with it, but we eventually adapt. This is the crux of why we eventually start doing — or not doing — things out of fear. Simple cause and effect. We get *conditioned.*

What I mean is this: if we don't grasp the rote memorization method of learning we are punished. If we do poorly at test time, we *fail.* If we give an incorrect answer we are wrong. If you give too many *wrong* answers you may be labeled slow, dense, stupid, or even worse. Of course this gets reinforced by those who love us most, and those we most want to please. Do you remember what happened if you came home to your parents with bad grades? How about when the teacher told your parents that "he's not working up to his full potential?" No one wants to be labeled a failure, so we do what comes natural in these instances. Right or wrong, we conform as best we can.

My point: it's very difficult for people to learn simply by reading, listening, watching, or being lectured to. Memorization of facts and theory does not necessarily help us attain our goals. That's why this book is loaded with practical assignments for you to do. It will not be enough for you to read this book if your goal is really to secure your financial freedom through Real Estate. This is a book of ACTION and practical APPLICATION!

The Number Two Reason Why People "Fail"

How about this idea of getting rich quick in Real Estate? Well, today you'll just have to call me *The Professor of Unrelenting Truth* because what I'm about to say is going to be **the most down-to-earth pitch for Real Estate and a Real Estate book you've ever heard!** The number of people who actually get Rich in Real Estate overnight is ridiculously low! Although I've taught literally thousands of people over the years—less than 100 got "rich" in their first year. The unadulterated truth is this: Rather than Get Rich Quick, Real Estate is *Get Rich Slow.*

This may not sound too exciting, but it took me three solid years of hard work before I could get out of the rat race and live off the proceeds of my Real Estate. No magic deal propelled me to a new stratosphere of wealth. On the contrary, it was a simple common-sense approach—more to do with persistence and motivation than with hitting the mother lode.

Early on, one of my business Coaches taught me this: successful people don't necessarily do three or four hundred different things to get rich. They actually do the same three or four things 100 times! That may not sound exciting. However, the people who do get rich in Real Estate—or any other business for that matter—do the same boring, mundane, and pedestrian tasks over and over, getting to the finish line way ahead of everyone else. *Then* they do the fun, sexy, high-flying deals!

So the number two reason people fail to succeed is simple boredom! While people believe there's a magical moment when really neat stuff is supposed to happen, it's really about *discipline.* Now don't start worrying if you're not the super-disciplined type. I'm a free spirit too, and there's nothing I like less than having to actually *do* something. In other words, I don't have any discipline or will power, either! I hope you

15

find that a relief, since it's all turned out pretty well for me.

What Tom Sawyer Taught Me About Real Estate

If you're lazy like me, the principles in this book will be your ticket to utmost financial freedom. The ultimate success secret in Real Estate is really about getting other people to do all the work, while you put together the deals and coordinate everyone else's efforts. I didn't have any burning desire to do Real Estate because I thought houses and apartment buildings were cool. I really just wanted the end result from owning all those houses and apartment buildings — lots of money! Frankly, it's not the love of green paper with pictures of dead presidents keeping me going, either. It's the **lifestyle I want to live**, requiring money as the fuel!

I don't have a construction background, a real estate agents' license, or a law degree for reading and writing contracts. What I do have is the ability to get everyone else working for me. Remember the story of Tom Sawyer whitewashing the fence? Remember how he got everyone else to do the work of painting the fence for him? Well that's what we do in Real Estate — and everyone benefits! Realtors make a commission when they sell us a property, so they happily find us deals. Banks make interest on our mortgages, so they happily pay for our deals. Contractors make money only when they're fixing up houses, so they do it for us. Property Managers make a percentage when they find us a tenant and collect the rent so they do it for us. Our tenants want safe, comfortable, affordable housing so they pay the rent, which in turn pays for the mortgage, taxes and insurance on our property. The money left over after all the bills are paid is my profit and provides me with the money to afford my lifestyle without working, so I keep buying more houses. It's a win–win–win–win situation!

The beauty is, with everyone else expending all the effort and providing the bulk of the expertise, I can stay focused on the three or four things I need to do 100 times to be successful at Real Estate. If I can do it, you can do it, too! So if you'll agree that doing the three of four boring things you'll have to do to get Rich might be worthwhile, read on. You'll discover what it really takes to get Rich in Real Estate and you'll have a **Tactical Action and Implementation Program** to get it all done for you.

Chapter 2: Taking Control

Control Only What You Can Control... Namely, You!

Control Only What You Can Control…Namely, You!

You're reading this because you want to make some money in Real Estate. Or maybe you want to have a new career—and make some money in Real Estate. What this tells me is you're not as happy as you could be with what you're doing now—your lifestyle—and how much money you're currently making—or not making.

If I were to meet you in person and ask you how come you're not living the lifestyle you want, you'd probably tell me you're not yet making the money you want or need to make right now. I'm also sure you'd have some really good reasons, like:

- You were born into a family without a great deal of money, so your parents couldn't help you much.

- You don't have a college degree, so you can't get a high paying job.

- You're so busy keeping up with life and kids, you don't have the time to pursue another career track.

- You've had a bad car wreck—or some other similar problem—and it's ruined your finances, your credit and your health.

- Plenty of other good reasons.

None of that's your fault. Let's face it. Things happen and sometimes you don't have any control over them. And those things have shaped your life and have gotten you to where you're at right now.

But let's think about the future.
No one's life is perfect. No one's life has ever has been per-

fect, and it won't be in the future. Let me say it very directly: bad things could happen to you in the future. It's a fact of life. You can't control other people — if your spouse decides to divorce you, if someone burns your house down, if someone sues you... you can't control what other people do.

But you **CAN** control you.

Now, I'm not saying you can always get out of the way of the bad things — they still may happen. What you can control is how you prepare for them and react to them. And in a larger sense, you can control what you choose to do with every aspect of your life.

Let me give you an example: two old widows lived side-by-side in two old wood-frame houses. Their names were Annie and Sally. One night the wiring shorted out in Annie's attic and her house caught on fire. The fire spread to Sally's house. Both women got out OK. As they sat out on the curb, across the street, they watched the firefighters battle the blaze.

It became clear that both houses were burning to the ground. Both the women had insurance, but Sally was crying her eyes out. "I don't know what I'm going to do," she wailed. "I've lost my home. I have no home. I'm homeless."

Annie, however, was smiling. "I've been looking for a reason to move out of there, and I didn't have any money. Now I'll have to! I'm sure looking forward to getting a new home. I didn't really want it to happen this way, but there it is."

Let's think about this. The same exact catastrophe happened to both women, and they both had the same means to deal with it — insurance — yet one of them chose to get upset and see it as a disaster, while the other was able to see it as the opportunity she'd been looking for.

You can't prevent things from happening, but you can choose how you respond. You are in control of you. You may not think so right now, but trust me — you control you.

What We've Been Programmed to Think

We learn more from our mistakes than from our successes. That may seem cruel, but it's true. It probably has something to do with our primitive caveman days, when the dangers were very physical. If you didn't run when the saber-toothed tiger roared, you were dead.

So people tend to take bad experiences to heart much more intensely than good experiences. Remember ever burning yourself on a stove? How long ago was that? That long ago, yet you still recall it. That event made quite an impression on you, didn't it? Now try to remember a good meal you or your spouse cooked a month ago. Drawing a blank?

That's what I mean. Although it's a bad trait to have in modern times, we humans are too often conditioned to allow the negatives to steer what we do far more than the positives.

Because of that, most people raise their kids in a very risk-averse kind of way. They teach them nice, safe strategies. Your own parents may have raised you this way. Go to school, get good grades, don't cause trouble, go to college, get a good job, get married, stay married, have kids, and pay your taxes.

Your parents taught you all that because they loved you and wanted the best for you, and they truly believed that keeping you away from risky behavior was the best way to keep you safe. They probably got it from **their** parents, who raised them the same way. It's an attitude learned from the Great Depression, when money was very scarce. Back then most people didn't take risks with money because if they lost any they'd starve.

The good news: If you follow that advice, you may get into the middle class. The bad news is that you'll **stay** in the middle class. You may have what many people believe is a nice, safe, secure life. Not much will change, and if it does change unexpectedly, hopefully you'll have some type of insurance to cover it. You'll work hard for your money, and then re-tire—if you can, at today's prices!—on a modest income, live in a little house, fish, and eventually die.

What's the problem with this scenario? Many things, but let's just focus on the money. You will always—and I mean ALWAYS—be working for money, chasing that buck, digging for those dollars. People work for money because they've been taught it's the honorable, upright, moral, hard-working thing to do. This "truism" has been propagated since the be-ginnings of the Industrial Revolution. This is…

The Big Secret of "The Rich"

People who own businesses actually need most people around them to be willing to work for money, because those are their employees. The business owner generally has his money working for him. The same thing goes for the inves-tor—someone who finances businesses and other ventures—he has his money working for him.

Now what do I mean by "money working for him"?

Well, it's called **passive income.** Passive income is money you get in the form of profits from things you own, without your having to do work. Donald Trump has plenty of pas-sive income from all the Real Estate buildings he owns, so he gets huge checks every month. If he wasn't an ambitious man, he could just jet around the world all the time, going from party to party. He doesn't have to work—his money works for him.

I know what you're probably thinking: "Well, sure, that's fine for those who can. If you've inherited a million bucks, you can buy Real Estate and get big checks. Where am I gonna

24

get the capital to do that?" But that's the great thing about Real Estate. You really don't need much capital to get started. We'll study that in depth later. Read on.

Being a business owner or an investor is like owning a money-printing machine—you own something that makes money for you, without you even being there.

The Rich, the Poor, and the People in Between

"The Rich are different from you and I," goes the old saying. It's true. Not just because they have more money than most, but because of how they interact with their money. What does that mean? I'll explain.

But first, let's learn a few terms the Rich use to help them make money.

- *Income* is money that comes to you. If you have to work for it, it's called active income. You got the money from an activity performed by you. If you don't do the activity and your income flows from things you own, like a patent on the intellectual property of a piece of machinery, it's called passive income. Examples: your paycheck is active income. Rent checks you get from a duplex you own is passive income.

- *Expenses* are money you owe each month, but not from assets (see below) that you own—they're from things you rent or use. Typically, for services like utilities and gas, and for rented things like apartments or furniture. Examples: phone bill, rent, newspaper subscription.

- *Assets* are things you own. Assets may or may not produce income, but they are things you can sell if needed. They also have intrinsic value, meaning they

25

are definitely worth something! An ounce of gold is a non-income producing asset because nobody sends you a check every month just because you own it. A duplex is an income-producing asset because people do send you checks every month for living in it. Appreciating assets get more valuable with time, like gold or Real Estate. Depreciating assets get less valuable over time, such as cars that are not collectibles.

- *Liabilities* are generally things you need to pay for because you own them. If you own a car and it's financed, the car itself may be an asset, but the loan on it is definitely a liability.

Now that we have working definitions for some key concepts let's take a look at the way different groups of people use these words either for or against themselves.

Poor People

First off, I make no apologies for using the word poor. When I started my journey on the road to financial liberation, my wife and I shared a poor person's financial statement. We rented a two bedroom apartment in Northeast Philadelphia. We both worked, we had no savings, and we had mountains of credit card debt. We bought used cars on monthly payments, we had basic cable, used water and electricity sparingly and we ate scrambled eggs for dinner every night. On the weekends we put cheese on our scrambled eggs to make them taste better. We had the financial education of the poor, so we had to find our way out of the rat race from the position of the poor.

Now, let's start by taking a look at the **behavior** of poor people. Poor people are poor because they don't make much money, right? Not quite. They are poor because they don't own much. Generally they don't own their home, their car, or their employment. The only assets they tend to have are their security deposit on their apartment and maybe a small amount in savings. On the other hand, they have plenty of payments they must make, like the rent, the electric bill, the telephone bill, a car payment, and maybe a few others.

So the poor tend to work for a paycheck, and Uncle Sam takes taxes out of it before the money earned can be spent. The money is then spent making payments for rent for their housing and on their car. Maybe even their furniture!

That's why poor people *stay* poor. Their income doesn't go up much and they never own anything. When they get old, they'd better have some family to care for them because if they don't work, they don't have income.

Their income is active, meaning they work for it. They have no assets, and thus, no liabilities, but they have plenty of expenses.

Poor people have:

• Income (active)

• Expenses

Middle-Class People

Now, what about middle class people? They're better off, right? They've got all that wonderful home equity because early in their careers their parents or someone whispered to them, "Buy a home. It's the best investment you can make."

And it was… Up until about the 1990's. Then all the big banks started looking around for new ways to get money, and they realize that there were tens of millions of middle-class families who had lots and lots of equity in their homes. And you know banks—they're in the business of loaning money. They prefer to have their loan secured by an asset, so why not your home equity? So they started a big advertising push to get people to turn all of that equity loose. The banks called this new loan a debt consolidation loan, or a second mortgage, or a home equity loan. Unfortunately for the American Middle-Class, this advertising was very powerful and inviting.

It's worked so well there's a special name for it: "The Middle-Class Debt Trap." You know how traps work; they lure you in with some juicy, tempting bait. In this case, the bait is credit card debt and home equity loans.

Here's what happens: Joe and Susie Middleclass get married. For a few years, they rent a small apartment. They both have good jobs, so they make decent money and they save a lot of it. They're very proud of themselves.

Then they decide to have a baby and they take the conventional advice and buy their first house. After all, it's the American Dream, right? Now they're not saving as much, what with the baby expenses, the mortgage, and having to buy yard equipment, furniture, blinds, lamps...all sorts of stuff for the house. And then there's peer pressure—their friends all go on nice vacations, drive SUV's and wear stylish clothes, so of course Joe and Susie have to do that, too. It's called "Keeping up with the Joneses."

Their choices aren't the best, so their debt mounts. Finally, they realize they're in trouble, just barely making their bills each month. Their savings are almost zero. So they consult a financial planner. He smiles. "The smart thing to do is consolidate all this debt under a home equity loan. Your payments will be lower and so will your interest rates. Oh, and by the way, don't run up your credit cards again, it's just not a good idea."

That sounds like really good advice, so they do it.

At that point, they could still come out of debt OK, if they minded that last piece of advice and left the credit cards alone or better yet, cut them up.

But they have all these friends, and Susie's sister just called and wants to know if Joe and Susie can go to the Bahamas again this summer. How can Susie say no? So they haul out the credit cards and start using them again.

Pretty soon they've maxed out their cards again. Now they're worse off than before: same credit card payments, same first mortgage payment, same car payments — and, on top of everything else, now they also have the new home equity loan payment.

The only option left is bankruptcy or a drastic overhaul of how they view and use money.

Middle-class people may be somewhat better off than the poor because their income is higher. However, it's still active income and taxed to the max.

What dooms most middle-class people these days is that they typically convert an asset — home equity — into a liability by taking out home equity loans. Then they go and make things much worse by adding a lot of expenses to their financial burdens by running up their credit cards.

Middle class people have:

- Income (active)
- Expenses (boy, do they ever!)
- Assets (what's left of home equity and a few paper investments, like a 401k and maybe some mutual funds)
- Liabilities (huge ones, usually associated with homes, cars and credit cards)

What you need to learn from this scenario: Assets are

things you own that pay you money, whether you work or not. Liabilities are things you own that you have to pay money to own, or because you own them.

By the way, debt is not necessarily bad. I have millions of dollars in debt, but I control how I use debt. For example, if I take on debt for an investment property that's bringing in more money than I have to pay on the debt — that's called positive cash flow. Debt is bad when it's something bringing you no money, like credit cards with high interest rates. Learning how to use debt correctly is one of the most important skills for a Real Estate investor.

Wealthy People

By now you're probably wondering what it is, exactly, wealthy people do differently besides being born into money...or maybe marrying into it. Well, on Forbes Magazine's 2007 list of billionaires, 60% — over 550 on a list of 932 — made their fortunes from scratch. That means they weren't born into wealthy families. Michael Dell, Ross Perot, and many others weren't born into wealthy families, so it can be done.

But first, here's what the wealthy do differently.

Wealthy people own things. Not just things that sit around and look nice, but things that bring in money for them. Things like apartment buildings — maybe you live in one right now. Things like office buildings — maybe you are reading this in one right now. They also turn these things into businesses.

That's why wealthy people have lots of income, much of it passive income. They can run off to the Caribbean for two months, come back, and the businesses they own are still humming along, making money. They probably do have some payments, but most wealthy people will choose to own rather than rent, unless there's a tax benefit, whenever possible, so mostly they have assets that create their income and some liabilities.

Their assets include Real Estate, companies, treasuries, stocks and perhaps wine and art. The passive income from assets pays for all liabilities and payments and then some.

Wealthy people have:

- Income (passive — they don't work for it)
- Expenses (all paid for by the passive income)
- Assets (large ones that produce the passive income)
- Liabilities (paid for by the passive income)

Note that the wealthy pay for their expenses and liabilities by using passive income. Unlike the middle class, they are **not** going deeper into debt each month, since passive income pays for all their expenses and liability payments. So how did wealthy people get to that point? Stay tuned!

Who's Who in the Income World

I'm not going to try to tell you there are two types of people in the world, because actually there are really four types. As far as how you get your money and how you live, there really are just four categories.

The Employed

This is probably the category you're in right now. Employed people include office workers, engineers, store clerks, truck drivers...anyone who works for a paycheck. Employed people work for money they receive from their employer.

However, what they really get are leftovers. That's right,

leftovers! Thanks to the federal government's tax laws, Uncle Sam gets his cut of your check first, before you even see the money. It's called Withholding Tax. You may be shrugging, thinking, "So? They do that to everyone. Big deal."

Well, no, they **don't** do it to everyone. Would you believe business owners only pay taxes on what's left over after all their bills are paid? That doesn't happen for you now, does it? Nope. You have to try to pay all your bills on what's left over after the government gets done taking out what it wants. Sure would be nice to only have to pay taxes on what you don't spend, wouldn't it?

Well, you can! And I'll show you how.

The Self-Employed

Self-employed people are typically pretty proud of being self-employed. After all, they don't have to work for "The Man." They don't have to live in a cubicle, take a drug test, or show up for work at 8 AM if they don't want to. They're their own boss…sort of.

What do I mean by "sort of"? Well, there's still the matter of the customer, and any businessperson who doesn't realize the customer is the ultimate boss isn't going to be in business for long. Self-employed people include plumbers, lawyers, doctors, accountants, consultants…anyone in business for themselves who does the work themselves. These people are also called solo-preneurs, or sole practitioners.

Self-employed people still work for money, like employees do. But they are somewhat better off than employed people because if they're smart and clever, they can form a one-person company like an S Corporation or a Limited Liability Company (LLC) that allows them to pay all their business expenses first and then be taxed on what's left over.

However, self-employed people aren't true business owners even though they might like to think they are. Why not? Because the acid test of a true business owner is this: if she went off to Europe for a one-year vacation and then came back, would the business still be running? Profitably? Think about the plumber — who fixes the faucets and toilets if he's off in Europe?

The answer: if the self-employed person goes on long vacation, becomes disabled or even has to take a sick day, the business stops. If the business stops, there's no income. Period. And if the self-employed person took off for a year, when he came back there would be no business to come back to.

Thus, the self-employed still work for money.

The Business Owner

The true business owner not only doesn't have to do the work, he doesn't even have to be there every day. Why not? Because he owns a system and he's hired people to do the work, and hired very smart people to supervise the workers, and hired even smarter people to run the whole company. Thus, in many cases, the president of the company works for the business owner.

If the business owner went to Europe for a year and came back, he'd probably find that his business is still up and running, and hopefully even more profitable since a year has gone by.

Business owners do not work for money. After initially investing in a business idea, and a business system, they let the money they've invested — which is now in the form of a business — work for them.

The Investor

The investor is similar to the business owner, except his money doesn't come from owning a profitable business. His money comes from an investment in a company — usually as a silent partner or a limited partner with his ownership represented by stock — an investment in a Real Estate partnership or company, an investment in the development of a product or service company that pays a royalty or distribution of profits, and a wide variety of things.

The investor's job is to provide the "at risk" seed money for an entrepreneur or business owner to develop an idea or build a business that will in turn generate cashflow from a successful implementation or application of the idea or business. But the same principle applies to the investor as with the business owner: his money works for him. He won't be doing any of the work. He'll simply fund the work getting done. There's no good reason why he can't take off for a year and come back, and see his investments are still making money for him.

Sound like that's impossible for you? Well, take heart — you CAN get there from wherever you are right now! Obviously, you're not going to jump from being an employee to being an investor overnight. But what you can do is start taking the steps to move from an employee to self-employed, then business owner, and then — if you'd like — an investor.

Done right, Real Estate can be your vehicle for doing all this! How can you use Real Estate to achieve huge levels of passive income? Well, that's what I'm going to show you next.

Chapter 3: Living the Dream

The Road from Poor to Wealthy

Living the Dream—The Road from Poor to Wealthy

I hope you've learned from my book, so far, even though your life until now may not be everything you want, it doesn't have to stay that way. You are in charge of you. You make the decisions that will affect the outcome of the rest of your life.

Do you want to stay where you're at right now? Do you want to work for money all your life? Do the middle class thing? Get in debt? Have to get a home equity loan? Then get even deeper in debt? Maybe even have to declare bankruptcy?

Or do you want to make a decision, right here and right now, to start laying the foundation for building wealth— **real wealth**? Wealth that will eventually provide you with enough passive income you don't have to work for anyone else...**ever**! I made that decision. Let me tell you how it's worked out for me.

My Story and How It Relates to You

To give you some perspective on why I'm qualified to be telling you how to get from where you are to where you want to be, let me tell you my personal story. Pay special attention to the parts you can see yourself in. I'll bet you'll find a few. Most of us are really quite similar. We want many of the same things, and many of us believe the things we want are out of reach. Well, I'm living proof using Real Estate as a vehicle worked for me. And if it worked for me, it can work for you, too. I'm really no different than you. I may be wealthy and successful now, but that wasn't always the case.

When I was in school, I was a real trouble-maker. I got my first detention in kindergarten for blowing bubbles in my milk, and when the teacher told me to stop, apparently

I didn't listen well enough. My mother had to patiently wait in the hallway while I served out my half-hour detention sitting at a desk with my hands folded. Things didn't get much better from there.

By the time I got to high school, I had been through five schools, suspended or expelled from each and every one. I was fulfilling the prophecy the grown-ups around me had pronounced as my fate; "He's a bright boy, but he doesn't live up to his potential."

My life is pretty much an open book and I have nothing to hide. I hope that by telling you my story I can make a positive impact in your life if you've had some of the problems that I've had and you're concerned that you can't be successful because of who you are, or where you're at right now.

I started drinking alcohol when I was just 11. It began with a little peer pressure and swiping a bottle of Jack Daniels from behind my dad's bar. I'll never forget that night. I was sitting under the deck of the family pool; Mom and dad were out bowling for the night.

A few swigs of the magic juice and I suddenly felt like I fit in. I was outgoing and funny and people liked me. That was the complete opposite of who I was for the first 11 years of my life. By the time I was 13, I was already a full-fledged alcoholic. That's how I ended up bouncing from school to school during my teenage years.

By the time I was 17, my parents were demanding that I straighten out, so I joined the US Army Reserve. I had high hopes I could turn things around since the old emptiness I felt inside had returned full force and no amount of mind/mood-altering substances could take that away.

After eight weeks of basic training at Fort Dix, NJ, I was a new man—for the next few weeks, anyway. By the time I finished my secondary training at Ft. Eustis, Virginia, I was right back where I started, drinking every day and wallowing in self-pity and despair.

Within a month after I left the military, I was jobless, friendless, and living on the streets of Philadelphia. I spent the next year trying to figure out how I became homeless, I wasted every day feeling sorry for myself, despairing the world's cruelty, wanting to be someone else, and wishing I were dead.

Fortunately, I have not felt that way for many years and now I love being me and having my life. But it was a tough road getting there, and quite a few people showed me a lot of love and support at a time when I couldn't love myself. I thank them now.

You see, there was a turning point—the day I finally decided I was sick and tired of being the person I had become. A day I decided there was more to life than being spiritually bankrupt, beat up, and alone.

That day, as I was sitting underneath the elevated train at Bridge and Pratt Street in the Frankford section of Philly, an elderly woman wagged her finger at me and told me I should be ashamed of myself for wasting the **opportunity of life** my Maker was kind enough to give me.

My first reaction was anger. I wanted to tell her off. But then it dawned on me in a blinding flash, she was right. I was squandering my opportunity to be "more." Instead of wishing I was more, I could actually do something about it! So I did.

I like to call this an "Aha Moment." That's the moment you know things can be different for you—and you become willing to do "whatever it takes" to make everything different. Despite my lack of luck and the fact I did not grow up well-off or well-educated, I've had the great fortune to become luckier than most human beings ever get to be. And I have the added benefit of really appreciating that I'm no longer where I used to be.

As a result of that chance meeting with the old woman under the Frankford El train, I went to college. Since I was paying for it myself — with loans and grants — I actually paid attention. I also challenged everything that didn't make sense to me. Just because a professor said something, I didn't automatically assume it was true. I've found this habit to be very useful in adulthood, although I still find it challenging when my kids do it. I also had the good sense to work while I was in college and I used that money to immediately pay off my loans. Then I was able to stop taking the loans and pay outright for my classes. That gave me a lot of freedom when I finished school. The only debt I had was for the last semester's housing bill, just a few thousand dollars.

For many young folks, college debt is an absolute killer, literally. They have $50,000 or more of debt to pay back, but they can only get a $30,000 job. Then there are taxes, living expenses, and, heaven forbid, recreation! The age group with the highest rate of suicide in America is 22-23 year olds. I think we're overlooking some obvious connection. Drive past your local college or university on a Saturday. One of the first things you'll see is tables set up outside every campus recreational area. Do you know what those tables are for? Getting college kids to fill out credit card applications in exchange for freebies, like T-shirts, and towels, and Frisbees. The average college kid leaves school with close to $10,000 worth of credit card debt!

I started my first business (a "failure") at the age of 26. I was just married and already sick and tired of going to work every day. I failed that business — a pay-per-minute political opinion hotline — because I didn't know how to market it. But my second business was in the computer industry. I turned that business into a multimillion dollar a year company. However, it was still a job. I had employees, but I was the bottleneck. As a certified control freak, I was personally involved in almost all aspects of the business, especially service delivery. So, I worked 12 to 14 hours a day, seven days a week. Even vacations were limited to once every two years—always planned at the last minute—because I never knew what would happen next.

The business cycle kept repeating and I couldn't make it stop! Make a sale, install a computer network, turn over the documentation on the network and get people trained. Then I'd realize that we had no cashflow and have to start the whole process over again. Somehow, business expenses and taxes always rose to the level of sales and income.

After a few years of this never-ending cycle and my repeated promises it would all be over in just a few short years, my wife took me on one of those "forced vacations." Workaholics and A-types know what I'm talking about. That's when your spouse tells you "That's it! Pack a bag! We're going on vacation, or we're getting divorced!" Don't get me wrong. We had a lot of nice things. Nice house, nice cars, nice stuff, private school for the kids, cleaning people, etc. We just had no time together!

While I was packing for my vacation I had a choice of books. I could bring the new John Grisham book, about 400 pages long with little, tiny print—or I could take the book sitting on my night stand for the better part of six months, *Rich Dad, Poor Dad,* by Robert Kiyosaki. What caught my attention was the book's subtitle, *What the Rich Teach Their Kids About Money That the Poor and Middle-Class Don't.* As soon as I saw that, a light bulb went off in my head. "Aha! I knew there was something they weren't telling me!" Besides, that book was less than 200 pages long, the font was big, and it seemed to be written on a fifth-grade reading level. I was hooked!

I read the entire book cover to cover on the flight from Philadelphia to Jamaica. What I learned from that book was profound, and somehow, in 16 years of school, the lesson was never taught! I found out the Rich don't do what they rest of us do. The Rich buy assets that throw off income they don't have to work for. Their motto is, "Work once, get paid forever!" I also learned an amazing definition of wealth by R. Buckminster Fuller, inventor of the geodesic dome. You know, that giant golf ball-looking thing in front of Disney's Epcot Center? His definition of wealth: *How many days forward you can live from this day, maintaining your current lifestyle, without working for income.*

So, what does all that have to do with Real Estate? Well, it was the exact moment of my awakening to the possibility a world might exist that I knew nothing of. This event also set the wheels in motion for me: I realized someday I could be a productive member of society, financially free, liberated from the shackles of money.

That moment, it finally became obvious to me that becoming Rich was NOT about becoming a millionaire, but instead about a very attainable goal! I only needed to find out what my monthly expenses were, and then replace that income with money that I could get *by not working*! This was a total relief. I had monthly expenses of about $5,000, including recreation. That meant I only needed about $5,500 per month in passive income—totally achievable as a money goal... by anybody!

Sitting on the beach in Jamaica, I announced to my wife, how, when we got home, I was going to sell my technology consulting company, take the proceeds from the sale and invest it into income producing Real Estate. She looked at me like I was crazy, but after I explained to her what I had just read, she agreed. I wish I could say that the rest is history, but it wasn't.

I do admit it hasn't always been an easy ride. Over the years I've experienced my share of ups and downs along the road to financial freedom. I've never let myself get discouraged, despite having had about a half-dozen previous businesses that failed. The biggest lesson I've learned in going from bum to businessman is this: *losing is a part of winning.* Losing gives me the opportunity to learn, as well as something to compare with the joy of winning. And nothing's ever a total loss if you can learn something from it. This book will make it possible for you not to repeat the mistakes I made. Therefore, its value to you should be in the tens of thousands of dollars. Not the $15 or $20 you may have paid for it!

How I Got On the Right Track

So back to our story of the Really Big Lesson. My wife and I returned home and I was excited to get started on my new Real Estate adventure. I called a business broker I knew and asked him to list my business for sale. Within a few weeks we had two offers. The first was for less money than I was asking, but I didn't really mind. It was a seven-figure number — since I had started the business with only $2,000, the price seemed fair. It would be plenty of money to start investing in Real Estate. There was a catch, however. The buyer insisted I stay on with the business for three more years as an employee. Needless to say, that's not what I was looking for, so I rejected the offer.

Offer number two was right behind the first. This offer was for more money than I was asking! I was very excited and arranged to meet with the buyer to discuss his offer face-to-face. We met at my office on a Wednesday morning. He was an older gentleman who looked like he'd been in business for quite a long time. We went through his offer line by line. I was very excited until we got to the end of the meeting, when he informed me his offer was contingent on me staying on with the business for five years after the sale. Five years? I wanted my life back! I challenged the man and asked him why.

He informed me I owned what's called a "key-man" business. I asked what he meant by that? He quickly and politely explained without me, there was no business. So I didn't own a business at all. I owned a job! Gently, he informed me I was trying to sell him a job. He didn't want a job, and obviously I didn't either. He recommended if I insisted on not being part of the sale, I should learn how to build a system to create *recurring revenue* from the business and then call him back. At that point he might be interested in owning the business without me present.

I was quite upset. I wanted to start investing in Real Estate right that second. I wanted to be done with the technology business forever. And I certainly didn't want to do the work to fix it before I could sell it. Then, in a flash, a new idea entered my mind. I'd do both! I'd start investing in Real Estate for passive income, and I'd systematize the technology business so it could eventually run without me. I no longer had to decide either/or. I could do both! And that's exactly what I did.

On that journey, I learned what it takes to go from Loser to Winner. I developed formulas and systems that consistently deliver results required to do Real Estate successfully — to deliver passive income. I found coaches and Mentors to teach me the essential business skills I lacked. Over the years, I've shared these systems with thousands of other people too, and many of them have become quite successful as a result.

Despite hearing my story and seeing my current results, there's still one thing that keeps people from taking that next step... one thing that keeps people like you and me from having the things we really want in life. Even once people decide that the leverage, the tax benefits and the passive income from Real Estate are what they want...above all else, they still can't make it happen. Just one thing keeps people going back to work instead of going to the beach...

What's Holding You Back from Financial Freedom?

"The only thing we have to fear is...fear itself." Franklin D. Roosevelt said that, and it applies to investing in Real Estate more than any other phrase I know.

I give workshops, teach classes and coach people through the first steps of investing in Real Estate. And when I do, I ask people what's holding them back from buying that first piece of investment property. While I get a lot of different answers, they all say pretty much the same thing. These are the most typical responses:

- "I'm afraid I'll buy a bad property and lose money."

- "I'm afraid it will cost more to fix up that property than I thought and I'll lose money."

- "I'm afraid I'll get bad tenants who trash the place and I'll lose money."

- "I'm afraid the market will go south and I'll lose money."

- "I'm afraid I'll fix up a house and no one will ever buy it from me and I'll lose money."

- "I'm afraid there will be extra costs I don't know about and I'll lose money."

- "I'm afraid someone will sue me over my property and I'll lose money."

- "I'm afraid I won't know what I'm doing and I'll lose money."

Get it? What holds back potential Real Estate investors is FEAR. And it's almost always some sort of fear associated with MONEY.

The number one reason why 90% of all people who buy Real Estate books and go to boot-camps never buy a SINGLE piece of investment property is **FEAR!**

So let's just get this out in the open: yes, risk is associated with investing in Real Estate. You **could** lose money. And if you do enough deals, you probably will — at some point — lose some money, but you'll make far more on your other deals than you lose on the occasional not-so-good deal.

What you need to know is this: risk exists throughout your life! Do you think having a job and working for money is risk-free and secure? I know plenty of ex-dot-com employees who would tell you otherwise. Let's face it: there's no such thing as company loyalty anymore. That went out back in the 80's.

Employees today job-hop frequently. Companies know this, so they don't feel the least bit sad about laying off people who have been with them 10, 15, even 20 or 30 years. There's no such thing as job security anymore.

And there's yet another reason for investing in Real Estate, particularly for those of you under the age of 55. What do you think will happen to the Stock Market, and to your 401k plan, when all the baby boomers begin retiring around the year 2011? What happens to the Stock Market when everyone starts pulling money out? What happens to Social Security when 75 million baby boomers retire?

What happens in a market when you have far more sellers than buyers? What will happen to any Stock Market investments you may have when that time comes? And who will be in charge of the government at that time? Do you trust them? If the markets crash, who will be looking out for your interests?

And then there's the matter of taxes. If you're employed right now, do you really enjoy the government taking their cut out of your paycheck before you even see the money —

and then they just toss you whatever is left over? How does that make you feel, having to make do with the leftovers from your paycheck? There is a better way, I promise you.

My point is not to scare you—but to make you aware that you—*and only you*—are responsible for your own financial well-being.

Your finances are like a lifeboat. You can choose to buy a lifeboat in the form of a 401(k), mutual funds or Stock Market investments. But when you buy a lifeboat already built, you don't really know how it's put together or how well it will hold up. You have to trust the people selling it to you. However, when you build your own lifeboat in the form of a Real Estate empire, you know exactly where all the money comes from, so if you get a hole in your boat, you know exactly who can fix it, and how.

Real Estate empires are not just something Rich people have. Plenty of plain, ordinary people just like you and me are taking steps right now to build our own lifeboat to financial freedom.

This is not just a "Rich Man's Game." People have been investing in Real Estate for hundreds of years. The first book I'm aware that teaches about Real Estate investing was written in 1758 by Benjamin Franklin as a prologue to his *Poor Richard's Almanac.*

Real Estate is for everybody and it's for you, too. In the next chapter, we'll start taking the steps together to build true wealth and financial freedom for you and your family.

But first...

The Real Estate Lifestyle 7-Step System™

Now you understand the vital need to build your own financial freedom through Real Estate investing, so we're going to get down to the nitty-gritty. The system I'll walk you through, step-by-step, is so easy an eight-year-old could do it, if they'd let kids buy property.

My trademarked system consists of seven steps. I'll list each of them here now, and then in later chapters, we'll explore each step in greater detail. Along the way, of course, I'll give you real-world examples with real numbers so you can see exactly how it all works.

Step 1: Get Financing — You'll get some capital, either from your own accounts or equity in your home, or from private investors, or from a bank or hard money lender.

Step 2: Find Properties — You'll go through listings and select properties that are good candidates for investment.

Step 3: Assess Properties and Estimate Repairs — You'll do a walk-through of the properties you've selected, assessing their condition, and estimating how much money it will take to repair them to marketable condition.

Step 4: Make Offers — When you see a property that looks profitable, you'll make an offer. You'll learn to run the simple math, so you make offers that profit you.

Step 5: Close On Properties — You'll buy the property.

Step 6: Fix Up Properties — After you've bought the property, you fix it up to make it attractive to prospective buyers or tenants.

Step 7: Execute Your Exit Strategy — Once you fix up the property, you sell it, rent it, or lease-option it to some one—and start making cashflow and/or passive income.

Don't forget, the Real Estate Lifestyle is a program of action, so your "homework" will follow each subsequent chapter, complete with a checklist so you can track your progress and see real results! Nothing is more important than actually doing what needs to be done. That's the most powerful way to overcome fear! You actually do it and find out you can!

*"Do, or do not. There is **no try**."*
Yoda, Jedi Master

Homework: Remember, R. Buckminster Fuller's definition of wealth: How many days forward can you live your current lifestyle without working. So, if you have monthly expenses of $1000 per month and you have $5,000 in the bank, you have a Wealth Factor of about five months. Let's start to quantify where you stand today because that will tell you how much money you need coming in from your assets each month to leave the rat race.

My Monthly Expenses:

My Mortgage Payment $ _____

My Taxes $ _____

My Real Estate Taxes $ _____

My Car Payment $ _____

My Credit Cards $ _____

My School Loans $ _____

My Child Care Payments $ _____

My Food $ _____

My Entertainment $ _____

My Spending Money $ _____

My Savings Account $ _____

My Investing Account $ _____

Other Monthly Expenses: $ _____

Total Monthly Expenses: $ _____

Monthly   **Passive**   **Income**   **Needed:** $
___

Is this Monthly Passive Income Needed number an amount achievable for you? I assure you that if you remember Real Estate is not "get Rich quick," but instead "get Rich slow," you'll achieve your Passive Income Number much faster than you think! What about inflation? Doesn't the cost of living always go up? Well let me ask you; have you ever heard of rents going down? Rents are generally indexed for inflation. What that means: rents rise at the same rate as the cost of living!

What if you want to expand your lifestyle? All you need to do is add more Real Estate income and you can cover it! No more "belt-tightening" for you!

Chapter 4: CYOA, Baby!

Cover Your Own Assets

CYOA, Baby!—Cover Your Own Assets

Rich people play the money game by a different set of rules than most people. The Rich protect themselves from creditors and predators before they start accumulating assets. We will, too. It's a tough world out there. You know it and I know it. You've probably heard a bunch of warnings from your family and friends about how you can get sued when you're in business.

I won't lie to you—it's true. You can get sued. Of course, you can get sued for anything at all at any time in America, the way people are these days. You could be walking down the sidewalk and look at somebody cross-eyed and get sued. Of course, just because you're sued doesn't mean the other side will win, but it can still cost you time and money.

My point? Risk is involved in nearly everything we do.

Do you drive a car? You could get in a wreck and be sued. Will that stop you from driving the car? No, because the benefits outweigh the potential risk.

The benefits you will gain from investing in Real Estate far outweigh the risks, so don't let the fear of being sued stop you. When you drive your car, you're protected by insurance. So, I'll show you how to set up a form of "insurance" to protect yourself and your properties.

The best way to protect your business and your properties is to make sure you set up a legal structure that protects you and your own personal assets from liability.

Now what the heck does all that mean? Let me tell you a story.

Jack the Pool Man

Jack was a guy who ran his own business cleaning and maintaining swimming pools. Jack wasn't too good with numbers, so he had a bookkeeper who took care of sending invoices and collecting money.

One day Jack asked the bookkeeper if he should set up something like an S Corporation or an LLC (Limited Liability Company) for his pool business.

"Nah," the bookkeeper said. "You don't need anything like that. It's too complicated, it'll cost you a fortune in lawyer fees, and it'll make your taxes a lot harder to figure out. You already registered your business, *Jack's Pool Service*, with the County as a DBA (Doing Business As). Just operate in a Sole Proprietorship, and it'll be easier to do your taxes."

So Jack took the bookkeeper's advice.

The next summer, Jack's business was doing so well he had to hire a helper. Jack was in a hurry so he hired a guy named Bobby who worked part-time at the pool supply store. He didn't take time to check Bobby's criminal background. That turned out to be a big mistake.

What didn't Jack know about Bobby? That Bobby was a convicted thief. When Jack sent Bobby over to a lady's house to clean her pool, Bobby stole her TV, silverware, and jewelry.

Bobby was caught and put in jail. The woman sued *Jack's Pool Service*. What Jack didn't realize was that Sole Proprietorships offer no legal protection whatsoever. So when the woman was awarded a half million dollars in damages, she was able to take Jack's house, his truck, and put a huge judgment on his credit report. The insurance company paid out a paltry $100,000.

Jack's wife divorced him when they lost the house and he wasn't able to get any more pool work. He had to declare bankruptcy and the resulting stress drove him to become a recluse. He lived out the rest of his days in a tiny apartment, working behind a counter for someone else, and spent his life a very bitter man. To this day, Jack curses lawyers.

The true tragedy is that it didn't have to happen this way. Had Jack been willing to pay lawyers and accountants up front for professional advice and a good business structure, he could have avoided his life being ruined.

If someone ever tells you there's no need to set up an LLC or some other form of entity to do Real Estate — and they will — just tell them, "You don't know Jack!"

Legal Structures for Your Business

If you're going to invest in Real Estate and you try to operate as a sole proprietorship, you could end up like Jack. If a tenant sues, and you don't have enough insurance, they can grab your home, your car, and all your money.

This is why corporations and Limited Liability Companies were invented — to protect against such threats. These legal structures also have some significant tax advantages. Remember how I said businesses only must pay taxes on what they don't spend? Well, that's true for corporations and LLCs, but not for sole proprietorships.

Let's say you're a Real Estate investor and you need to buy a new computer for your business. You budget $1,000 out of the profits from rents coming in this month to buy your computer. Let's also say that your tax rate is 25%.

If your business is a sole proprietorship, you'll have to lay aside $250 of that $1,000 to pay taxes. Then you get to buy your computer with what's left over.

However, if your business is an LLC or an S Corporation, that $1,000 goes straight into your business checking account.

If you spend that $1,000 on a new computer, you don't have to pay any taxes on it!

Now, I know what you're thinking—there's no free lunch. You can't escape the tax man. True, but you can put him on a diet! When you run your business as an LLC or S Corporation, you only pay taxes on:

1. Profits left in the business at the end of the tax year or quarter.

2. Money you withdraw for your salary or as an "owner's draw."

I want to stress none of this is illegal. This is all perfectly legitimate and on the up and up. You're not cheating the tax man; you're just taking full advantage of the law. The reason you can do this is because a corporation or an LLC is actually what's called a "legal fiction." It has all the rights of a person, except it's not alive. Corporations and LLCs pay taxes, they hire, they fire, they sue, and they can be sued, much like people.

Here's the big legal advantage: if your property is owned by your business—and your business is a corporation or an LLC—when someone wants to sue over a property dispute, they must sue the property owner. And that's the LLC or corporation, not you. Should the worst happen and they win, they can take things that belong to the LLC or corporation, including the property, but they can't touch your own personal home, car, or money.

What kinds of legal structures can you adopt for your business? Well, I'm going to lay them out for you now.

Sole Proprietorship

A sole proprietorship is the easiest legal structure for your business to take. **Unfortunately, it is also the worst.** Yes, it's simple to do your taxes if you have a sole proprietorship; you just add an IRS Schedule C form to your regular personal income tax form.

Your big problem is legal liability—you have no protection against lawsuits, just like Jack the pool man didn't. Also, it's very hard to sell a sole proprietorship, since the value of it is based on the owner, not the business. Typically, self-employed people like plumbers and electricians use sole proprietorships. But that's not you.

There's also a problem with inheritance. Sole proprietorships end when you die, so your heir can only sell off the assets. They can't sell the business as any kind of a going concern.

Don't use this structure for your Real Estate investment. It's the same as taking title to the property in your own name. Just don't do it.

Partnerships

Partnerships usually come in two types: limited and general. The limited partnership is also known as a Limited Partnership (LP).

General Partnerships are not usually a good entity to use for your business. Many people like them because they are very easy to form; all you really need is a handshake deal. The problem with an easy handshake deal is you have no written agreement on how profits will be distributed. When there is no such agreement written down, the law assumes you are 50–50 partners.

The biggest drawback is that each partner can be held personally liable for all the partnership's debts and actions. Even if your partner signed a business contract to buy something without you knowing about it, if you're in a General Partnership with them, you're on the hook.

And even though 50–50 sounds fair, you have to look at who brings what to the table.

Suppose two women, Linda and Sue, want to start a quilt-making business. Linda puts up $10,000 to buy supplies and a sewing machine and materials to start the business. Sue doesn't have any money, but since she has the quilt-making knowledge, she agrees to reinvest her first $10,000 in profits back into the business so it's fair.

Things go south. The women argue, can't agree, and Sue leaves town before they make a dime. Then Linda finds out Sue ordered a whole bunch of expensive material and brochures to market the quilts. Linda is now out her original $10,000 plus $2,000 for the items Sue ordered. Linda has to pay for that stuff even though she didn't order it. Not good.

Another bad thing about General Partnerships is that they end when **one** of the partners dies. This can leave the other one in the lurch. Also, if you ever want to sell the business, most savvy buyers won't touch a General Partnership since they have no idea how indebted the business is.

Don't use a General Partnership for your Real Estate investing business.

The Limited Partnership (LP) is a better arrangement. It has two types of partners: general and limited. The general partner is responsible for managing the partnership and can spend the partnership's money or take out loans. S/he is also personally liable for debts and claims. If you have more than one general partner, they are all liable; a creditor can go after one of them for all debts, or all them.

The limited partner is limited to putting money into the business and that's it. He gets to say he's an owner, but he

60

doesn't make any of the decisions.

If you want to hold property for your children, this might be an ideal arrangement, since they can own it but they have no say.

Limited Partnerships are also a good option for you if you are raising private money from other people to put into your Real Estate investments. More on that later.

Corporations

Many books have been written about corporations, because they can get pretty complicated. I'll keep it simple here and give you just what you need to know.

Corporations tend to start off as S Corporations and stay that way as long as possible, until the IRS makes them become C Corporations.

Here's the benefit to an S Corporation: profits you make above and beyond the salary you pay yourself can flow through the corporation without being taxed until they hit your personal income tax return. And even then, you do not have to pay the self employment taxes, Social Security and Medicare.

So, you avoid the double taxation of a C Corporation, in which the corporation's profits are taxed; then when you withdraw your part, you pay personal income tax on it.

Sounds great, right? Not so fast. First, you must follow some rules, or the IRS will revoke your S Corporation status and make you become a C Corporation, and therefore you will have to pay taxes twice on profits.

Here are the rules an S Corporation must follow to stay an S Corporation:

No more than 75 shareholders
No nonresident alien shareholders (must be a US citizen)
Must be a US Corporation, set up in any state but not outside the US
Cannot be an ineligible corporation (some business types are ineligible)
Only people, estates, and some trusts can be shareholders
Only one class of stock is allowed, but different voting rights permitted

There's one other important advantage: some states require LLCs to pay a franchise tax above a certain income level. Corporations usually don't pay this in most states. This varies from state to state, so check with a local accountant or tax professional.

Also, with a corporation, you will need officers and a board of directors.

Generally, the S Corporation can be a good entity to use, particularly if you think you might like to sell your Real Estate business in total at some point.

Limited Liability Company (LLC)

If I had to pick my favorite structure for a Real Estate investing business, it would be the LLC. Best of both worlds, they have members and can be managed by all them (member-managed), or by just one of them (manager-managed).

For your Real Estate business, you will most likely be a single-member LLC, so you will be the manager yourself.

There is no double taxation with an LLC—you pay yourself out of it by taking draws on it, and then you pay your own personal income taxes on those draws. For money left at the end of the tax period in the LLC, you pay taxes on that.

If you have other members of an LLC, you can divide up

profits and losses in a flexible way. For instance, if you contributed 20% of the start-up costs but you did a whole lot of the legwork in looking at properties, you could have an arrangement with the other members so you get 50% of the profits.

However, I must caution you, if you live in California, the fees for setting up an LLC, along with the legal maintenance, can be large. Check with an attorney.

The disadvantage to an LLC is if you happen to develop some great new Real Estate model and go to sell the company, venture capitalists don't much like LLCs. They prefer to buy corporations. You can convert an LLC to a corporation, but expect to spend a few thousand in attorney's fees to get it done. It's probably worth it.

And don't forget the franchise tax. Texas, in particular, imposes a franchise tax on LLCs of 4% on gross revenues of more than $150,000. If you're not making at least $150,000 a year, you don't have to worry about it. Just know it's there, lurking to snatch money out of your pocket when you're successful…

Land Trusts

Land Trusts are an increasingly popular type of legal vehicle. Since Land Trusts are fairly new, there are a few large loopholes that will probably be closed at some point. For now, however, it's a great way to protect your privacy.

They are a form of trust, but unlike most trusts, a trustee runs the show. If you, the beneficiary of the trust, want to spend the trust's money, you have to get the trustee's permission. And the trustee has to disclose your identity to anyone who asks.

Land Trusts are different. That trustee has no real power other than being a figurehead. You get to make all the decisions. Even better, the trustee is required by law not to disclose your identity to anyone unless there's a court order. Yes, a court order can bust open almost anything; nothing is foolproof. Otherwise, no one knows who really owns the property.

Why would you do this? Sometimes it's in your best interests to keep your ownership of a particular property private. Maybe you have creditors after you, or you're getting a divorce... For whatever reason, there may come a time when you need to legally hide your assets. A Land Trust may be perfect for that purpose.

But actually, the biggest reason to use Land Trust is for buying pre-foreclosure property. Property owners in pre-foreclosure — i.e., they've received a Notice of Default — are usually in other kinds of trouble. They've probably got plumbing bills and home remodeling bills they never paid, as well.

When you buy a property in foreclosure, it's common for you to get socked by liens Contractors keep filing against the property — and now those liens are your problem, unless you bought the property with a Land Trust.

If you've bought pre-foreclosure property through a Land Trust, you can keep these future liens off your property, thus avoiding costly litigation. It's much harder to sue you if they can't find you.

Another key benefit is that with a Land Trust, you don't have to sell the property — you just sell your beneficial interest in the Land Trust, since the Land Trust owns the property. So your name is not on the public record. It's not on the record with an LLC either — the LLC name is. Interestingly, the most common reaction from creditors' attorneys when they see a property is owned by a Land Trust is a very deep groan.

So, consider using a Land Trust if you're thinking about getting into purchasing pre-foreclosure properties.

Of course, there are advantages and disadvantages to all forms your business can take. To be absolutely sure, you should consult a tax attorney or an accountant. Be careful you have an attorney set up your LLC (preferred form) or S Corporation—do not try to do this yourself. Sure, you can pick up forms to file, but there are meetings you must hold—yeah, I know, with yourself, but you still have to do it—and forms to file yearly. It's called legal maintenance. Let an attorney do it.

A word about attorneys: Yes, they may cost you money. But if you think **they** cost, talk to someone who's been sued. That costs more, a whole lot more. There's a saying, "If you think education is expensive, try ignorance." Get a good Real Estate attorney who deals with property investors, and take him to lunch. Pay them their fees for drawing up contracts, and by all means ask advice of them and pay them whatever they charge you. It is well worth it to stay out of big legal trouble.

Homework: Right now, while you're thinking about it—go straight to your local Yellow Pages and schedule an appointment with an accountant. Ask for a 30-minute consultation (these are usually free) so you can review with him your current financial situation from an income perspective as well as an asset protection perspective. Be sure to get answers to the following questions:

1. Based on your current assets and income, which entity will provide you with the best tax position, while still giving you bullet-proof asset protection?

2. What will it cost you, in your state, to set up an LLC?

3. How long will it take for you to receive a copy of your Articles Of Organization from the state?

4. Will he provide you with a Corporate Binder, and a Corporate Seal? Or does he have a contact for you to order one?

5. If you've selected an LLC, will he be filing the Protective Election Form for you?

6. Will the accountant file form SS–4 for you as well?

7. What fees will the accountant charge for setting up all these requirements for your entity for you?

Based on the thoroughness of his/her answers, decide if this is the right person for you to work with long term. If not, interview more accountants, until you find the right chemistry and price mix.

Chapter 5: Getting the Cash

Let's Go Get Some
Other People's Money!

Getting the Cash—Let's Go Get Some Other People's Money!

Since many of the biggest fears most new Real Estate investors have tend to involve money, let me put your mind at ease right now. Getting the money to do your own Real Estate investing is much easier than you think.

Even if you don't have great credit, money is available from many different sources if you want to be a Real Estate investor—provided you get the proper vocabulary and preparation before you approach the bank. You'll be glad to know that getting money for your deals is the very first thing we'll be taking care of. Once you have your financing lined up, you'll be good to go on your very first deal.

Now, I know you're probably wondering, "But Jim... Where do I get that financing?" And you may be remembering the last mortgage loan you got, maybe for the house you're living in right now. It probably wasn't an easy process. Maybe you're renting right now or living with a parent and you're not scarred from the process of getting a mortgage. Well then, good for you. You won't be scarred—or scared—now, either.

Believe it or not, it's actually much easier to get money for investment Real Estate than it is to buy your own home. Why? Because the lenders know they're dealing with a business person, so there will be revenue coming in from the property in the form of rents to pay the mortgage, not based on your personal ability to pay the bank.

The wonderful thing about investment Real Estate is how the tenants will be the ones actually making the mortgage payments for you. Not literally, of course—you don't want to give a tenant a coupon book for the mortgage and tell them to pay it. What I mean is the amount of money you receive in rent should be enough to cover any mortgage on the property, along with repair and maintenance costs, property taxes, insurance, and, of course, a nice profit for you.

When I talk about getting financing for a property, I'm really talking about getting the cash to buy the house outright. Cashola—that's right, you got it!

You see, to get the best deals, we buy with cash. You know what I'm talking about. Cash is king. Money talks and everything else walks.

We buy the property with 100% cash—preferably with other people's money as described later—eliminating the need for a mortgage and all the conventional lending issues that many people getting into this business need to deal with. Mortgages have a whole lot of strings attached, so we avoid them. This way, we get to save our personal cash and we always have plenty of money available to do more deals.

OK, now, you may be a bit confused about where you can get tens or even hundreds of thousands of dollars to buy a house—and we'll get to that, I promise. For the moment, I'd like to explain our financing system first. That way you'll be able to see the big picture about what's going on, and why it works. And, most importantly, how you can make it work for **you.**

To handle our acquisition costs, we use a line of credit, a cash advance, a business loan, cash from friends and family, money from private investors, hard money, or any of a dozen other methods for getting the cash, to make the initial purchase of the property. Then we fix the place up and get the renters in. Now we own 100% equity in the property. No first mortgage, no seasoning issues—meaning, we don't have to hold title for a long time—or any other liens on the property. We own the house outright.

Our next step in the process is to line up the long-term financing with a loan from a traditional lender using the property as collateral for the loan so we can pay back our original lending source.

Consider, if you will, the power in this scenario. You are going to the bank **with collateral.** You are NOT like everyone else walking in hat in hand, begging for money. Many people in Real Estate come to the bank asking them to be their 80-90% partner in their deal, but they have nothing to offer except the down payment. There's no real incentive for the bank to treat those people as anything other than an "applicant." Remember — money follows management — so if you're walking in the door with a property you own "free and clear" the bank is far more inclined to be your friend. After all, you are now going to the bank with what they want most... **Real Estate.** Banks loan money on Real Estate faster, cheaper and much easier than they do on any other asset — even gold!

Types of Financing

Now that you understand how the financing system works from a 10,000-foot view, here's the rest of what you need to know. There are four basic types of financing you can arrange for the properties you're going to buy:

- Traditional

- Commercial

- Hard money

- Private money

Traditional Financing

As the name implies, traditional financing is the type of financing people use most commonly to get up-front working capital. There are a few requirements to use traditional financing, namely good credit or existing assets you can liquidate or borrow against.

Traditional financing comes in many forms. Here are the most common:

Home Equity Line of Credit (HELOC) — This is a second recorded mortgage you take out on your own home, or another property you own, to get the cash for buying an investment property. There are pros and cons to using a HELOC.

PRO:

- The biggest pro is it's easy to get. If you have a substantial amount of equity in your home, you can easily get a HELOC for a large amount of cash. And, after all, why let your equity just sit around and do nothing for you? Why not make it go out and work for you by buying an investment property. The line of credit is represented by a checkbook the bank gives you so you can make any type of purchase that you want.

- Using a HELOC, the money is generally very cheap. You can easily get a line of credit that costs the prime rate plus maybe 1-2%. After all, the bank has a really good chance of you paying them back.

- Finally, banks generally have HELOC products where you only need to make interest only payments while the capital is in use. So, if you borrow $50,000 from your HELOC, you only make a monthly payment of about $150 each month while the money is out — far cheaper than a mortgage payment. When you pay back the loan balance, your monthly payments stop.

CON:

- Your home is the collateral for the line of credit.

A second mortgage is recorded by the bank for the amount of the full line of credit. If you don't make payments, you could have big problems! To alleviate that risk, don't borrow more than you need to and make sure that you have some cash on hand to make payments while the rehab is performed and tenants are found.

Where do you get a HELOC? Any bank or credit union. Be prepared to have your credit checked, and be aware you'll need to have at least some amount of equity in the property you're using as collateral for the HELOC.

So, if you live in a house with a market value of $150,000 and you owe $145,000 on a mortgage, you find the total equity by subtracting $145,000 from $150,000.

Market value of property	**$150,000**
Amount owed on mortgage	$145,000
Total equity:	*$5,000*

Most banks and credit unions have a minimum on HELOCs and it is usually about $10,000. They also have a limit on how much you can borrow. Even if you own the property outright, the limit is usually 80% of your home's value. The phrase banks use for this is "Loan-to-Value," or LTV.

What LTV means is how much they'll loan you based on how much equity is in your home. If you've owned your property for a long time, or if you bought it with a lot of cash down, or if property values have gone up a lot where you live, you may have a lot of equity in your property.

Let's take that same $150,000 house and say you owe $60,000 on it. So now your equity is $150,000 minus $60,000 equals $90,000. If the bank is willing to do an 80% LTV HELOC, your numbers would look like this:

Market value of property	**$150,000**
Amount owed on mortgage	$60,000
Your equity	$90,000
80% LTV on the home value	$120,000
Amount of your HELOC	*$60,000*

In this case, the bank would give you a checkbook and tell you that you can spend up to $60,000. The beauty of any line of credit is that once you pay back the balance, you can use it again, over and over, until your Real Estate Empire is built!

Cash in the Bank — You withdraw a chunk of cash from your bank account and use it as the full payment for an investment property. This, of course, assumes you **have** a nice, fat chunk of cash in the bank.

The advantage: you're not borrowing money, so you pay no interest. The disadvantage is that it depletes your cash reserves until you refinance the investment property. For many people this is a far better use of their cash than any other investment venture they could find.

IRA/401(k) — You can take a loan from an IRA or 401(k) plan to buy Real Estate. This is a terrific option, and it's particularly advisable to do this before the Baby Boom generation begins to retire and cash out of the Stock Market. In other words, do it now while your IRA/401(k) is still worth **something!**

You want to do this in the form of a loan, since there are usually substantial penalties for cashing out an IRA or a 401(k), particularly if you are not yet fully vested at the company. In other words, you haven't been there long enough to get the full company match.

Now, you **can** own Real Estate in your 401(k) — it's allowed
by law — but the big drawback is that you are only allowed
to benefit from income (rents) and appreciation (selling at
a higher price). You cannot benefit by taking depreciation
on your taxes. Since depreciation is a major benefit to owning Real Estate, I don't always advise owning Real Estate in
your 401(k).

But it might be a good idea to borrow against your 401k to
get the cash to do a Real Estate deal.

Investment Accounts — If you have a private investment
account such as stocks, mutual funds, bonds, etc., and they
aren't doing too well, you can cash them out and use that
money to invest in Real Estate.

I know you might be reluctant to cash out those accounts.
Many professional people love to compare their investment
accounts like it's some kind of badge of honor. Well, let me
tell you, when the Stock Market is stagnant, as it was from
late 2000 through the summer of 2005, you probably weren't
seeing much of an increase in those investment accounts.

So why not just cash them out and stick that money in
something that **does** consistently perform, like Real Estate?
Your money can go farther and do far more for you. Why?
Because with stocks, bonds, and mutual funds, when you invest $5,000, you control $5,000 worth of stocks, bonds, or mutual funds.

But when you put that $5,000 down on a property, you can
control a piece of Real Estate worth $150,000 — how's **that** for
leverage?

Life Insurance — This applies to whole life insurance, not
term life insurance. What's the difference?

Term life insurance provides a fixed amount of life insurance as long as you pay the premiums every month. When you stop paying, it goes away. People under the age of 55 tend to own term life insurance and it is the type most employers offer.

Whole life insurance is an annuity you buy into, and you retain the value of it even if you stop paying. The amount of benefit it promises to provide rises as you pay into it, so it's almost more like a savings account in that respect.

You can't cash out term life insurance policies, but you **can** cash out whole life insurance policies. And you may have a whole life insurance policy without even knowing about it. Years ago, many new parents and grandparents routinely bought whole life insurance policies for their newborns so that if anything happened to the parents, the child would be provided for. A lot of people have found these policies in old safe-deposit boxes or home safes in their grandparents or parents homes. Ask them.

Credit Cards—This is a way to obtain a down-payment for a piece of property, but in all honesty it should be your last resort. If you go this route, check the interest rate on your card very carefully and read all the terms. Most credit card companies today offer very low rates at first, then after a year the rates go up.

And in the terms, in very small print, are usually some clauses saying if you are late on a payment or you go over limit, or basically do anything the credit card company doesn't like, your rate goes up—**way** up.

However, if you have a 0% APR card and you are very sure you can pay the money back with your refinance before the rate on the card rises, go ahead and take out a cash advance or write a check off the card if there is no other way to get the money you need to buy your first property and get on the road to financial freedom.

Personal Mortgage Loan — This is how a lot of people buy their first handful of properties. While this is the "conventional" method of doing things, I don't recommend it. By using a personal mortgage loan, you're going to go through the same process as buying a home to live in, except it won't be owner occupied, so you'll still pay the commercial rate for the mortgage. This is generally 2 or 3 points higher than a residential mortgage.

You'll also need all the requisite inspection and mortgage contingencies the bank wants in your agreement of sale. Imagine this scenario. You're a motivated seller and you want to be absolutely certain your property will sell the quickest way possible. One offer you have has a contingency (escape) clause saying if the buyer can't get a mortgage, or get the mortgage for an interest rate satisfactory to the buyer, the deal is off. The second offer you have is for cash, has no contingencies, and will close on Tuesday. Which one would you take? You got it — that's why we are the guys and gals with the cash!

Another downside to a personal mortgage is that you can only get away with this on your first few properties. You see, almost all home loans are insured by Freddie Mac and Fannie Mae, and those organizations exist to encourage home ownership.

When they see you have two or three simultaneous mortgage loans on your credit report, they will flag you as an investor. What that means is you won't be able to use personal mortgage loans to buy property anymore — you'll have to go commercial.

The final nail in the coffin for a personal mortgage is asset protection. We'll cover asset protection in detail later, but here's how a personal mortgage can hurt you. The bank will not let you take title to a property that collateralizes a personal mortgage in any other name than your own. No LLC, no Land Trust, no other entity. That means you must take the property in your personal name, exposing your name to the public record. Not only will tenants be able to find you there, so will every other predator and creditor. That's a good way to lose your first property as quickly as you got it!

The only upside to using a personal mortgage is that you can usually stretch out the term of the loan for 30 years if you want.

Where do you go to get a personal mortgage loan? Well, if you really have your heart set on getting a personal mortgage, any bank or credit union will do, particularly if you already have a good relationship with them. There are also many competitive online sources such as loanweb.com or lendingtree.com that allow you to use an online form to state what you want and then have mortgage companies compete for your business.

Commercial Financing

Commercial financing puts you into the realm of the true business person, right alongside the mega-superstars of Real Estate like Donald Trump and others. Commercial loans almost always exist only to fund investment property.

The good part is they are actually easier to qualify for than a home loan, since the lender knows rents will be coming in to cover the loan note.

The bad part is you will pay slightly more interest—say, a point or point-and-a-half—for a commercial loan. And the payments will be higher, since the longest term they like to offer on commercial loans is usually 15 to 25 years.

Where do you get a commercial loan? You must deal with a bank, since credit unions are not allowed to deal with commercial accounts or loans. But banks can be friendly places, particularly when they see you're going to be bringing a lot of money through their door.

Mortgage Brokers — Since commercial loans are only made by banks, and you may not wish to visit several of them, you'll probably want to make connections with a good mortgage broker. Mortgage brokers make it their business to know all the bankers around town, and all the available loans — or "loan products" as they are called these days — and rates.

Using a mortgage broker can save you time and get you the very best loan at the best rate.

Where do you find mortgage brokers? In the Yellow Pages or online. Do a Google search along with the name of your locality and you will probably find several.

Business Line of Credit — Similar to a personal line of credit. Lines of credit come in two types: secured and unsecured.

A secured line of credit is backed up by some sort of collateral you put up. That's' why it's called "secured," because the lender secures something of yours. There are many different types of collateral you can put up, such as:

- Jewelry

- Rare coins

- The title to a car or boat

- Gold or silver bullion

- Partial interest in a business or property

- An investment account

- Personal savings accounts

- CDs (Certificates of Deposit)

- Money Market accounts

Should you default on a secured line of credit, the lender keeps the collateral. Getting a secured business line of credit is an option if your credit is not so great or you're overextended.

An unsecured line of credit is similar to a credit card, since you do not put up any collateral—you're not borrowing against anything. And like a credit card or HELOC, you can take a line of credit—secured or unsecured—up or down.

Where do you get a business line of credit? Well, since credit unions aren't allowed to do commercial banking, you need to go to a bank.

Hard Money Lenders

My friends and I lovingly label hard money lenders "loan sharks." Hard money is a high interest loan you get that's secured by collateral in the form of the property you're buying. In return for loaning you the money to buy the property, the lender has a lien on the title to that property.

If you don't pay the money back, or if you don't make payments, the lender can foreclose on the property and take it from you.

To get a hard money loan, you'll generally have to agree to pay 5 points—or 5% of the property's value. If you get one of the popular new interest-only loans, your payments will be lower, but you'll pay a higher rate, like 15 to 18%.

You will also pay more fees and costs to buy and sell the property. Since you will sell the property for more than you bought it, you'll pay more Closing costs to sell, since Closing costs are a percentage of the home's value.

How does this work?

Let's say you find a house that needs some repairs. You go look at it, and you estimate that if it was all fixed up you could sell it for $100,000. I'll discuss how to estimate repair costs later on. It will take $5,000 to fix it up, and the owner agrees to sell it to you for $60,000.

Here's how the numbers play out on a $100,000 property:

After Repair Value	**$100,000**
Purchase Price	$60,000
Repair and Fix-Up Costs	$5,000
Loan Costs — 5 points	$5,000
Closing Costs to Buy	$2,000
Closing Costs to Sell	$3,000
Your Gross Profit	*$25,000*

Not a bad deal if you consider that without the hard money, you could never have done the deal to begin with. It only takes a few of these deals to never need a hard money lender again!

Now, this next section covers the way many larger Real Estate deals are done. I want you to take a deep breath before you turn the page, because this is one of those places where you need to take a "leap of faith" and trust me. This next method of getting money for deals is the one that really propels investors to the next level! Ready? Here goes....

Money From Private Investors

Private money financing is money you borrow but not from banks, credit unions, or "official" sources. This is money you borrow from your family, your friends, co-workers, or people you know or come in contact with. This type of financing can be some of the best financing available. So don't be lazy and skip over this part. This method is by far one of the best funding sources available!

In this day — when banks are only paying 4-5% for 20–and

30–year Certificates of Deposit, and many people are getting poor and even negative returns from the Stock Market — a healthy 12 or 13% return from a Real Estate investment becomes very appealing.

Who do you know with an underperforming IRA? A poorly performing mutual fund? Cash in the bank yielding modest interest rates? Lots of people! Do you know doctors and dentists? Business owners? Other professionals? These people are all great sources of private money financing.

You need to present your request as a business proposition, in a formal letter or proposal, with terms including what interest you will pay them. If they see you're willing to treat them in a respectful, businesslike manner and sign a note, they will be far more interested.

BONUS FREE DOWNLOAD

Visit my website at **www.livetherealestatelifestyle.com/ Resources** and there you can download a copy of my **Real Estate Lifestyle** *"Guide To Raising Private Money" Workbook.* This is a great document you can customize for your own needs. It explains to potential investors what you're doing in your Real Estate investing business, deals you have already done , or sample deals if you have none, and the type of returns you are willing to guarantee. This is the same document I use to raise money for my own Real Estate deals. It works for me and it'll work for you!

You can get your **FREE** copy today!

It's my way of saying "Thank You" for reading this book.

Homework: Decide which type of financing you will most likely need to get your Real Estate investing business started. Then... back to the Yellow Pages. Find the phone numbers for local banks and call them up and introduce yourself. If you'll be using a HELOC, ask for the current rates and the requirements for you to apply. Call more than one bank, and while you're at it call your current mortgage company, too. If you'll be seeking Hard Money, find your local Real Estate Investors Association, also called a REIA. There are always Hard Money lenders who advertise in their newsletters and come out to their meetings looking for clients to work with. Go to the meeting, introduce yourself, and interview several of them.

Finally, use Private Money! Go to my Real Estate Lifestyle website now at **www.livetherealestatelifestyle/Resources** to download your FREE copy of my *Real Estate Lifestyle "Guide to Raising Private Money" Workbook* by Jim Canale. Make a list of at least
10 people you can meet with to present your offer. Now the hard part... call them to arrange a face-to-face presentation

Chapter 6: Finding a Deal

*How to Find the Money-Makers
in Your Own Back Yard!*

Finding a Deal—How to Find the
Money-Makers in Your Own Back Yard!

Now it's time to start looking for properties to buy and fix up. The problem beginning investors have is....where? Where to look, where to go? How to begin the search process? Don't worry—I will lay it all out for you so you'll feel comfortable in knowing where to find the properties to do your deals.

We'll cover different property types, locations, and how to leverage the Multiple Listing Service (MLS) to your best advantage.

Thanks to the Internet and other communication advances, you can invest in property anywhere in the world. You can live in Oregon and invest in Florida, live in California and invest in Maine, or live in Iowa and invest in New Mexico. But just because something is possible doesn't mean it's a good idea.

As a new Real Estate investor, it makes much more sense for you to start in your local area. You know the neighborhoods, you know the economy, you know the people. And you can go over and personally check out the property with your own eyes, ears, and hands.

When I say "your local area," I don't mean properties within a 10-block radius of where you live. If you happen to live in Manhattan, for instance, I can assure you that you won't find many Real Estate deals appropriate for a new investor. The same applies if you live on a farm where properties are miles apart from each other.

So, if you live in either extreme—an expensive city or a rural area—you may not find many great opportunities in your own back yard. But I'll come back to this in a moment and show you how that won't matter. You'll still be able to become a successful Real Estate investor no matter where you live.

For now, let's assume you live somewhere in between — either in or close to a decent-size city. How can you pinpoint a viable market for investing?

The important thing to know is how income divides up your community. Remember, your greatest opportunities for long-term cashflow are in lower to middle-income areas. We call these "working-class" neighborhoods. These areas offer the best value for the dollar as well as the highest number of renters.

But what if you do live in one of those extreme areas — either out in a highly rural area, or in the middle of an urban area where Real Estate prices are out of control, like Silicon Valley, New York, or San Francisco? In either case, you may need to consider a market that isn't right next door, but not too far away, either.

If you live in one of these extreme areas, I can almost guarantee that within 75–100 miles, you'll find a market to meet your needs. Think about all those restaurant and hotel workers in New York and San Francisco — they have to live somewhere, and they're not going to drive more than 75 or so miles to work. Does that seem like a long way to travel? Does 75 miles *every once in a while* seem like too far to drive to give you the financial freedom you've only dreamed of up to this point?

Just how far away is that company you've bought thousands of shares of stock in? I hope I've made it clear that an hour-and-a-half drive is a small price to pay for the comfortable lifestyle Real Estate investing can bring you.

Where To Look

First, get a good map of your city or county, if you don't already have one. Take a close look at it, and if there are some areas you're not familiar with, ask a friend, or drive to those areas and check them out.

Driving around is one of the best ways to get a Real Estate education. When I first got started, I'd spend hours just driving around "lost" taking in all the various aspects of different neighborhoods — proximity to hospitals, places of worship and funeral homes. These driving- around sessions became the basis of my knowledge of the different neighborhoods in the city I live near.

Your best bets are going to be lower to middle-income areas. And by middle-income, I don't mean upper middle class areas, I mean **middle.** Why am I advising this? Because lower and middle-income properties are generally a fairly stable market. Just like everything else, Real Estate goes through boom and bust cycles, and you've probably heard a horror story or two from someone who lost his shirt trying to play with the big boys in the high-end luxury home market.

Here's a secret, though: the booms and busts you hear about in Real Estate are mainly in upper-middle-class and upper-class residential properties. Why are there no real busts in lower-income properties? Because, like the old Real Estate saying goes, "Everybody's got to live **somewhere.**" There's three basic human needs and they are food, clothing and *SHELTER!*

Think about it: even if the US economy takes a nosedive, and a lot of people end up poor, they've all still got to live somewhere. So maybe they leave their nice upper-middle-class home and go to an apartment, a duplex, or a rental house.

Lower-income properties also tend to be populated by service workers who make lower- end wages, which means rents tend to track inflation—they never go down. Consider this if you've rented before—have you ever received a letter from your landlord announcing, "Congratulations, your rent is going down?" I don't think so. On the flip side, rents in these areas don't go up a whole lot either. Maybe 5-7% each year.

Also, you are much more likely to find "fixer-upper" properties you can get good deals on in lower-income and middle-income areas. If you drive through these areas, you'll see boarded-up windows no one's bothered to fix, or crumbling porches, or peeling paint...stuff that just needs some basic maintenance.

Upper-middle-class and upper-class areas, people take care of properties much better, so there really aren't too many bargaining points you can use as leverage to get a good deal. And there's another factor working against upper-middle-class and upper-class properties: they cost a **lot** of money. I'm not trying to be crass, but if you're a typical person just starting out in Real Estate, you just don't have the cash to start trying to invest in high-end properties. And even if you do decide to do this someday, it's best to cut your teeth on lower-income and middle-income properties—trust me.

Since the goal is to be generating good monthly cashflow to replace our current income, lower-income properties can't be beat. They don't appreciate a whole lot in short time spans, so you won't make a huge profit selling them, but they can be your cash cow.

What middle-class properties are best for is appreciation, particularly upper-middle-class properties. Be aware, of course, as I mentioned, there will always be swings in the market. But if you want to invest in a property you can rehab and sell at a nice profit, middle-class properties tend to fill the bill quite nicely.

One word of caution, though; you want to avoid out-and-out war zones. You know the kind of areas I mean—*danger zones*. Every metropolitan area has them. If you go to drive through an area and you see street-crime activity, burglar bars on every window, and really trashy-looking properties, leave and don't come back. It's not worth risking your neck to have to go there and deal with tenant issues and property repairs. I mean, what if you got a call from the police saying drug dealers were in one of your units? Or that someone had been murdered? These things can happen if you're not careful.

Middle-class homes are what regular income people want to buy, people with secure jobs and maybe a child or two. There's a sense of security that comes from owning a home for people in this bracket. Depending on where you live the income level varies, but consider this person someone who makes between $75,000 to $150,000 per year.

Now, as for location, you don't have to live near your properties, but it's a good idea not to be too far from them. You'll want to have them within a reasonable driving distance so you can go check on them and make sure they're being kept up. We'll talk more about that, as well as how to never **have to collect the rent, fix a toilet or make a repair…ever,** in a later chapter.

If you see an area on a map or get a tip about an area that sounds good, get in your car and drive around there. Notice what kind of place it is, what sort of vibe you get. Is it a run-down area with no new construction or renovation whatsoever, with elderly tenants and a high vacancy rate—lots of "For Rent" and "For Sale" signs out?

Or is it a semi-run-down area being renovated and upgraded? A sure sign a run-down area is turning around: when you start seeing upscale coffee shops and little boutique shops going in. That means the area is probably re-gentrifying, and if you can get in on the ground floor of that trend you can do very well.

As investors, we don't go where opportunity has already happened. We are looking for the area where opportunity is about to happen! These neighborhoods look quite a bit different than those that have already turned. It may be the area right next to the one that has just turned! I call these *fringe areas.*

Drive around several areas and jot down notes. These areas are your "farm areas" for properties. And don't just drive through them once. Do it several times, once every week or two, for a few months, so you get a good feel. Why not park the car and walk around the neighborhood a bit. That gives you access to a closer view than you get in the car. You can also talk to people out doing things in their yards or on the street and find out who's considering selling and what they think of the neighborhood.

Part of your selection process for your farm areas will depend on what you plan to do with the properties. If you're planning to fix and hold, then rent them out, make sure you pick properties in a strong rental area, with many other rentals. This ensures you'll get tenants coming into the area looking for units to rent. Lower-income properties are great for this.

In lower-income areas you can find all sorts of tenement or apartment buildings or duplexes, triplexes or quads to buy, rehab, and rent out. Just make sure the crime rate isn't at the point where thugs are going around kicking in doors.

If you're planning to fix and sell for profit, then you want to focus on areas where there are strong sales and prices are going up, up, and up. These would probably be middle-class properties, since they appreciate in value more than lower-income properties. Again, the Internet is a great source of information for community data: crime statistics, rental rates, census info, and neighborhood reports.

In middle-income areas, look for either nice single-family homes or duplexes. A duplex is a two unit home, sometimes referred to as a twin. We prefer single family homes and call these our "bread and butter" homes. That's because these homes tend to be what the typical family is looking for. Remember, vacancy rates are much lower in single family or row homes that have a decent amount of living space available, while your average duplex splits the same amount of space to create one or two bedroom apartments. Generally, we seek out homes with better than 1100 square feet of living space. So, look for a nice single family home, and you're on your way.

What and Who to Look For

When you go out looking for properties, there are many ways to find them. These are the methods I prefer.

- Working with a Realtor who brings you deals.
- Working with a Realtor who gives you leads on deals

Now you'll notice I didn't suggest you hang some "We Buy Houses" signs, and I didn't tell you to go to an auction or a courthouse, and I didn't tell you to send out letters to folks in foreclosure. You can certainly do all those things. However, Real Estate is supposed to be a Lifestyle Business...remember? If you make the process of finding deals totally labor-intensive and dependent on you personally, you may get out of the Rat Race, but you'll NEVER have any time of your own. You'll always need to be chasing your next deal.

Instead, you'll want to call in a Realtor to do that heavy lifting and deal finding for you.

The thing I like best about Realtors is they work for free. You don't have to pay them a cent unless and until you actually close on a property they either find or sell for you. So get some referrals from other investors, or just start asking around, for Realtors who will find you investment properties.

When you do find Realtors, you'll need to interview them. What you're looking for is a Realtor with a good attitude who's willing and eager to feed you listings. Don't expect that Realtor to drive you all over town to look at every single property they give you a lead on—be willing to go look at them yourself. Just ask them to feed you listings.

Your Realtor should be your ally. Once you've started a good relationship with them, and they get to know you better, they should have a very good idea what you're looking for in terms of property. Since they're exposed to all sorts of properties, they're in a great position to spot those properties you're looking for.

I'm not just talking about the property they personally see in their day-to-day lives, either. Real Estate agents have access to the Multiple Listing Service, or MLS. The MLS is a vast computerized listing of all property for sale through virtually any Real Estate agency. Your agent's usefulness isn't limited to just checking the MLS; he or she can create automatic notices that trigger when a property meeting your criteria becomes available.

If you are thinking you can just use some online service like Realtor.com to send you automated listings, think again. Too often, those resources get listings late, and the criteria you can use to sort through them aren't nearly as good as what agents have available.

Buyer Alert! Sometimes hot properties NEVER get listed on the MLS or these other resources, because the agent has contacted a potential buyer directly without even bothering to list it.

So, the only way to ensure you get the most up-to-date listing information AND position yourself as a "hot buyer" of investment properties who an agent will dial up first before even listing on MLS, is to establish a strong relationship with an agent who's always looking out for you. Make sure you treat your agent like a friend—because he or she is your friend in the Real Estate business.

When you meet for lunch, pick up the tab. Take a personal interest in your Realtor and understand what makes them tick. If they're good at what they do, they may represent several investors. Which one they call when a great deal pops up may just come down to whom they like the best. Make sure that's you.

Hint: It never hurts to remember people during the holiday season with cards and gift baskets, and it's also a great idea to send a thank-you note and gift whenever your Realtor finds you a property that turns out to be a great deal—after, of course, you've done the math and checked the cashflow.

When you deal with Realtors, make sure they know you want to set a contract deadline of 30 days on your Agreements of Sale. This gives you enough time to either do the due diligence on the property or wholesale it to someone else.

Consider giving bonuses to your Realtor when he or she does a great job for you. You could set some kind of criteria—say, if you close a certain number of deals they brought within a certain period of time, they get a bonus check.

What should you expect to pay the Realtor? Well, in most states, for residential property it's 3% to the Buyer's Agent and 3% to the Seller's Agent, or 6% if the same agent does both. For investment property, it varies, but you pay NOTHING when you are on the buying end of the transaction. The person who sells the property pays the commissions to the Realtors.

When you search for properties, what you really want is

a motivated seller. In the Real Estate world, you often hear that term a lot. But here's the thing: *all* sellers are motivated sellers. If they weren't motivated to sell, they wouldn't be selling. What you're really looking for is a **highly motivated seller.**

Why? Because a highly motivated seller is more likely to cut you a better deal, which could mean you get the property at your price, your terms, or both.

So what kinds of people are highly motivated sellers?

- People transferred by their company to another city, so they need to sell their house. They also need cash for moving expenses, since companies usually don't pay enough on a relocation to cover everything.

- People in foreclosure or other kinds of money trouble — these sellers' motivation is to avoid foreclosure. People buying or building a new house and they have to sell the old one to do it ASAP — they need a quick and reliable Closing.

- Growing families with twins or triplets, or empty nesters. If the sellers are retiring, they may want the security of a check in the mail every month, and thus may be willing to finance your deal. If they are moving up to a larger home, they probably want a quick and reliable Closing.

- Real Estate owned by the bank (REO). Lenders or government agencies who have foreclosed on a property and want to get it sold.

- People with poor credit whose Adjustable Rate Mortgage (ARM) payments keep going up again and again. Or they may have a balloon note due soon that they can't find financing. These sellers are trying to get out of a bad financial situation, so they need to sell now!

- People going through a divorce. They need the cash so they can each buy or rent a new place — it should be obvious they need cash, and they want a fairly quick Closing to get rid of a place with bad memories.

- A widow or widower whose husband or wife has passed away so they don't want to live in a home full of memories. This seller may finance your deal, since they may want a reliable monthly source of income. They also probably would like to close the deal fairly soon, although it may take them some time to gather and pack all their belongings, since older people especially tend to have accumulated lots of things in their homes.

- The adult child of an elderly homeowner who has either passed away and the child can't pay the taxes on the property, or the elderly parent needs to go to assisted living and the child needs cash to pay for it. These sellers are usually just looking to raise some quick cash, as well as sell the property.

You must understand what a seller needs — because motivation is just another word for need. All sellers sell their property because they **NEED** something else more than they need that property.

If you approach the deal from the seller's point of view, while still keeping your own best interests in mind, you can fulfill that seller's needs, and then your chances of doing the deal go up.

When you go to look for a property, here are some criteria I suggest:

- Single family home

- 3 bedrooms — this means the property will be attractive

to families, and families tend to be stable tenants since they want a stable environment for their kids.

- At least 1,100 square feet—nobody wants to live in a little bitty cracker box.

- One or more bathrooms.

- List price of $150,000 or less. Remember, we won't be paying the asking price!

Of course, multi-units can be great, too, since you can spread out your risk of vacancies. The biggest challenge is finding a highly motivated seller. Owners of multi-units tend to be other investors, like you, and they are usually savvy enough to have avoided getting into the position of having to be a motivated seller. Still, it happens, and it happens often. People's kids get sick and need operations, people get divorced, people have car accidents, so it is possible to get good deals on multi-units. But remember, your chances of getting a good deal are much higher with a single-family home—so focus on those highly motivated sellers for now.

Using the Multiple Listing System (MLS)

If you can gain access to the MLS system, through your Realtor, you can search for properties based on certain criteria. Let a Realtor do this work for you. I prefer the Realtor to do the work, since I'm a big fan of using other people's time (OPT) instead of my own. Here are the keywords I recommend using in your search:

- Motivated seller
- Bring all offers
- Fix-up/TLC

- Estate or POA (Power of Attorney)
- Bank owned
- Corporate owned
- DOM (Days On the Market) Look for more than 45 days, even higher in a sluggish market.

TLC means the property is a "handyman special" and needs some "tender love and care," just another way to say "fixer-upper."

Effective Time Management

Going out to scout for properties isn't just about driving around aimlessly. That's not efficient. Before you go out to look, you need to have an idea of where you're headed. Take an hour to read through the MLS listings. Set a goal to look at 50 listings, and search for the keywords I included above, along with DOM (Days on Market.) Get your yellow highlighter out and select 20 to 30 properties to check out.

Then, list in hand, go out and spend an hour doing drive-bys and look-sees on those properties. I'm not talking about going in—that comes later. Just driving by, looking. You want to inspect the exterior of these houses for any problems or structural damage. Does the roof have a big hole in it? Roofing can be expensive to replace, and if that hole's been there a while you're looking at mold and mildew problems and probably some nasty carpet.

Is the foundation cracked? Stay away. Are the windows boarded up? No big deal. My point: you can tell a lot just from driving by slowly or parking for a minute and jotting down some notes.

After you've done your drive-bys, narrow your list down to 20 properties you'll go back to and tour the inside. I know

20 might sound like a lot, but you won't get to look at all them, I promise. Why not? Because some of them will have been sold by then; some will have tenant issues that don't allow for showing; and some of them will have problems getting you a key.

So you'll probably end up looking at 10 homes. Plan to spend four hours doing this on a Saturday or Sunday, since it will take 15 minutes to look at each place and at least an hour for travel and getting in and out of places. Be prepared to make a cash offer on the spot. Why? Well, this goes back to why I recommend buying with cash.

A motivated seller is trying to get out of a bad financial situation and needs cash. The seller's probably already seen a lot of would-be Real Estate investors come through, mumbling something about offers contingent on bank financing, or asking him to do seller financing. News flash: motivated sellers don't like uncertainty and they couldn't care less about getting a check in the mailbox for some paltry amount each month for the next 20 years—what seller financing does.

The motivated seller needs cash. Listen to the benefit of my experience. When you're doing a deal on a distressed property, you can usually get a good price or good terms—but rarely both. When you go in there waving cash, figuratively speaking, you can get your price more often than not.

Back to time management. Plan to spend three to four hours a week going around looking at properties. The more time you spend, the faster your business will grow.

Homework: Get on **www.Realtor.com** and find a few Realtors in your area who specialize in investment properties. Now call them! Explain you buy one house a month on average and you'll be paying cash. That's what Realtors like to hear.

Then ask the Realtor to e-mail you all the listings in your area that meet your determined market criteria. For example; 3-bedroom, 2-bath homes priced between $1 and $150,000. You want them between 1100 to 1500 square feet in size, and you want those listed for 45 days or longer. Ask for an entire Zip Code. Review these listings, looking for the keywords we discussed earlier—motivated seller, TLC, fixer upper, etc.—and then do your drive-bys.

Next, call or e-mail the Realtor to schedule your walk-throughs of these properties. You should have 10 to 15 decent candidates, so do all your walk-throughs on the same day.

Chapter 7: Roll Up Your Sleeves

*Determining Value and
Estimating Repairs*

Roll Up Your Sleeves—Determining Value and Estimating Repairs

Once you've located a few possible properties you might want to buy, you'll want to get a number for the After Repair Value (ARV)—how much you can sell that property for after you've bought it and fixed it all up.

> **Here's my hard and fast definition of ARV:** "If this property was in excellent condition, what is the maximum amount a buyer would be willing to pay, today, to own this property?"

Figuring out the ARV is very, very important because it can make or break your profit. Those of us in the business live and die by this number. If you estimate it wrong, you'll waste time making offers—they won't be accepted because your offers will be way too low. Worse yet, if the ARV is too high, refinancing the property will be a challenge, unless you leave your own money in the deal—since you will have paid too much for the property!

What's the number one defense against miscalculating the ARV? Know your area! Don't try to scout for properties all over the place—find one or two of your "farm areas" you can spend time getting to know, well. You'll get a feel for what properties are selling for in that area. Once you do that, you'll be able to estimate the ARV better.

The ARV also drives what we're willing to pay for a property, since it determines the Maximum Allowable Offer (MAO) we'll make. We use a simple formula, tried and true, about 50 years old, to determine what we need to pay for the property.

We'll cover that in a later chapter.

There are three ways to determine the ARV. They all involve looking at comparable properties that have sold lately, in the same area as the property you are considering. We look at what they sold for. This is called getting "comps" and here's how you can do them:

1. **Online** — You can get bank estimates on the internet from these sources:

- www.ditech.com — Free E-Appraisal
- www.bankofamerica.com/loansandhomes
- www.domania.com/homepricecheck/
- www.zillow.com

Many other banking websites also offer this type of information. These websites provide a quick way to determine value. However you should never rely on these sites as your sole way of gathering information to determine the ARV.

2. **Quick Realtor Comps** — Any Realtor can do these for you, and they will do it for free.

- Settled Properties (6–12 Months) up to 0.5 miles

These are recently sold properties within a few blocks, up to a half mile, of the one you're looking at. This is the next best method of getting comps because the figures are fairly accurate. This information comes from the public record. However, most systems are generally 3–4 months behind, so this information will likely be dated by the time you go to settlement. This is especially true when Real Estate values are rising or falling rapidly.

3. **Long Realtor Comps** — These are the best possible comps to use. They are labor- intensive for your Realtor to produce, so use these after the property is under agreement and you're in the home stretch. You want these comparable properties to be:

- Located within a one block radius, up to three blocks maximum.
- 90 days old — Pending and Sold listings only.

You should get three comps close to what the property you're considering is like. The comps will list square footage, number of bedrooms and bathrooms, and amenities like garage and fireplace. Most importantly, it will list the price those properties sold for.

Take the top three home values of the comps, and that's what your house would sell for in excellent condition, also known as the ARV.

Estimating Repair Costs

Now that you've determined the ARV, you'll need to go out and look closely at those properties. By "look at them" I mean do the whole drill: drive over there, walk through the place, scrutinize everything so you can estimate what it takes to rehab them.

This is not the time to get squeamish. I'll be frank — sometimes you're going to see some pretty nasty things. I call this the "Squalor Factor." By squalor, I mean dirty, smelly, moldy, ugly things. You'll see broken windows, dog messes, holes in floors, mouse droppings, houses without landscaping, and you'll smell some really bad smells. But you know what? When you find out what a bargaining point things like that are, you'll learn to actually look forward to seeing a messed-up, trashed property, because you'll know you can use that as leverage to get a really good price. To me, those things look and smell like money!

What you want to watch out for is letting your emotions ruin the deal for you. Sure, that property might be a dank, dreary, depressing place that you don't want to even spend 15 minutes in, let alone own, but use some imagination. Picture it all cleaned up, with fresh paint — nothing smells as good as fresh paint — new carpet, and some TLC. Always assess with your head, not with your emotions.

Remember, YOU won't be doing the work. You'll be working with an experienced General Contractor who knows exactly how to do those repairs. No matter how ugly and disgusting the toilet you're replacing is now, a new toilet at the hardware store costs exactly the same price. We're looking for motivated sellers — and nothing motivates a seller more than not getting any offers on their property. An ugly house wasn't always an ugly house. As far as I'm concerned, it doesn't need to stay an ugly house.

There's a flip-side to this as well. Just because a property is pretty inside does not mean you've necessarily found a great deal, either. Investors don't look at a property and decide that since the walls are blue, and since that's our favorite color, we should do a deal. We care only about the numbers. Remember, the property is a cash register to you. Don't shop as though you are going to live there. You already have a home. If you buy based on emotion you'll become a motivated buyer and even a motivated seller won't cut you a break.

So, please, use the keywords and do your drive-bys. If you do, use your head. Many of the properties you look at, you'll want to make offers on. But sometimes you'll want to make an offer on a property that's too much trouble for too little, or even a negative return.

Here's an example of a property that's too much trouble;

The ARV comes in at $50,000. You go in there and see a fire's put a hole in the roof and scorched the walls. It will take $15,000 to put on a new roof, repair structural damage, replace the drywall and electric, install new carpet and appliances, and paint the place. You start at $15,000 for repairs, but we also have our costs to consider, such as taxes and Closing. Suppose those costs are $1,500. If you paid $37,500 for the property, that means you'd sink $54,000 into a place only worth $50,000—no deal at all. Now, if you could get the place for a steal, like $27,500, you could make $6,000 if you sold it after it was repaired. But you'll definitely need a motivated seller to accept that offer.

Soon enough, you'll get quite proficient at making decisions to make an offer or walk away. Our next chapter, **Making Offers,** will provide you with the formula I use to determine what to offer for properties. With this simple formula—based on 5th grade math—and your common sense, you'll quickly know when you should make an offer and when you should walk away. But we can't decide what to offer until we decide how much the repairs will cost, so let's carry on.

To estimate repair costs, use my handy Rehab Price Estimator. I've included a sample copy on page 150 of this book for your own use. You can download an electronic copy from my website to customize for yourself at **www.livetherealestateli-festyle.com/Resources.** How I got the cost numbers for my Worksheet was by meeting with various General Contractors and getting prices from them for various items I expected to run into regularly. In a short time, my list grew to a full page, and I formulated the Rehab Price Estimator in this book that you'll use again and again. You'll be amazed how easy it is to estimate repairs with a list like this. Remember, you do not have to get the numbers perfect! The General Contractor will give you his proposal for the work before you close on the property, so you will have plenty of time to get the numbers right before Closing on the deal.

The most important point to remember when inspecting a property is that you're looking for problems you'll have to pay to fix.

Major items you should look for during your property inspection:

- *Termites*—These dark brown, black-winged wood eaters are the property owner's worst enemy. You can check for termites by poking around the basement and crawl spaces with a big screwdriver, looking for damaged wood. You should also check along the foundation both inside and outside. It also doesn't hurt to check the areas around the property, too. Termites in an old tree stump or scrap woodpile are a bad sign. Termites leave an easily recognizable mud trail on the joists and exposed wood in the basement, and they love damp places. If you see evidence of termites, I recommend that you hire a professional termite inspector for about $100 to do a full inspection. If this is one of your first few properties, then I recommend moving on to the next property. Let a more seasoned investor deal with the headaches and unknown variables that termites cause!

- *Dry Rot*—Contrary to the name, dry rot is caused by moisture. It usually can be caused by condensation buildup, leaks that never got fixed, and faulty ventilation systems, among other things. The end result is a fungus that eats away at wood and wallpaper. Keep an eye out for fungus, mold or any other type of decay. Dry rot is typically found around garages, doorjambs and window sills. We're not afraid of dry rot though. New wood is cheap!

- *Foundation* — A couple of tiny cracks in the foundation are not usually anything to worry about. However, a crack of four or more inches could be a sign of serious trouble. Also, a sagging or leaning roof can be a sign of too much settling in the foundation. When you are new, I recommend you walk away from these types of properties, too. They can be very expensive to fix.

- *Roof* — How can you tell if the roof is worn? If the property is roofed with asphalt shingles, look for a lack of granules on the shingles. With slate shingles, look for chipping or discoloration. City properties are usually flat roofs. We look for holes and what we call "alligatoring" on the roof. Alligatoring looks like it sounds — like an alligator's back. You'll see this on rubber roofing which hasn't been applied correctly. On the inside of the property, a water stain on a wall or ceiling can be the sign of a leaky roof or maybe an air handler gone bad. Never, ever, ever pressure-wash a roof! I see people cleaning their roofs with this method and I guarantee you they are cutting the shingle life in half.

- *Brick Structures* — In some areas, brick structures may be limited to the chimney. In other areas, you may find whole buildings made of brick. In either case, check for crumbling or discolored mortar that will have to be re-done. This is called brick-pointing and can be very expensive if you have to re-point the entire building.

- *Septic Tank* — If the property has a septic tank, be sure to check the ground around the tank. Thick grass can be a sign of poor absorption, which means costly repairs. Generally a smell test can determine a problem — walk the drain field with your nose wide open and see if there are any foul odors. You can't just inspect a septic tank —

typically an inspection involves a cleaning because if you open it up you might as well clean it. If the septic system appears to be older, you might consider buying a home warranty and paying for the extra coverage because a drain field and septic system can be expensive to replace.

- *Driveways and Parking Lots* — Does the parking area appear to be in reasonably good shape? Remember, it doesn't need to be perfect. However, major potholes or drainage problems can be a problem.

- *Windows and Screens* — Make sure all windows and screens fit properly and are in good repair. A small, nearly invisible hairline crack in a window isn't a major concern — you can either replace the glass, or not, while a knocked-out window must be replaced.

- *HVAC* — Sometimes pronounced "h-vack", this stands for heating, ventilation and air-conditioning. Don't necessarily take the owner's word all's in order here. Fire up the heater to make sure it gets hot. Then fire up the air conditioner to make sure it gets cold. Check the age on the air compressor. If it's beyond seven years old, you probably have an $800 bill coming your way some-time in the next two years. Check the age of the air handler. If it's over 10 years old, you may be buying a new one soon.

- *Plumbing* — Check under sinks, around toilets, and the bath tub for any signs of moisture or rotting; signs that can indicate plumbing leaks in need of repair. Also check ceilings and corners below where the major plumbing items are, such as bath tub and toilet. Discoloration there means that there is, or was, a leak.

- *Appliances* — If the property includes any appliances,

verify they're in proper working order. Turn on the stove and see if it gets hot, open the refrigerator, run the washer and dryer...you get the idea.

- *Electrical*—Exposed wires in the garage or crawlspaces can be signs of old, inadequate wiring. Also, verify that the property is equipped with 220-volt service for larger appliances, such as some dryers and air conditioners.

Of course, you're probably no expert in home inspection. If you do spot potential problems, don't worry. Your General Contractor (GC) will be walking through the property for a formal Rehab Proposal before you buy the property. He'll verify the exact nature of the problems in the property. Actually, depending on how much you know about properties, you might want to pay a General Contractor to come with you on your first few property inspections. You'll probably learn a lot!

One last point on property inspections: if the property is already a rental, you'll want to consider the tenants, too. This can be both an objective and subjective evaluation. You'll want to look at whether they are taking reasonably good care of the property. You'll also want to decide if they seem like they'll be troublesome or not. And of course, if they're already in a lease, you want to see that lease once you have the property under contract.

Homework: Get your blank copy of the Rehab Price Estimator from my Real Estate Lifestyle website **www.livetherealestate lifestyle.com/Resources** and then set up face-to-face meetings with a few General Contractors. Bring along a blank copy of the Rehab Price Estimator and ask the GC to help you fill in the dollar values. What will the average window price be? Although he can't know for sure without measuring the window, but what is the average price of a regular bedroom window? Now, how much does it cost to remove the old window, put in the new one, and reinstall the window trim? Write that number in the "per unit cost" blank. Continue this process until the sheet is completely filled out.

Now test your Rehab Price Estimator by scheduling walk-throughs. When you're walking through properties, count the number of windows, doors, etc. to be replaced. Add them up and you should have your repair estimate. Next, get the Contractor to walk through the house with you and give you his estimate. Offer to pay $50 or $100 for his time and go with him. Don't disclose the number you came up with until he's completed his estimate. You'll see it's well worth it, and you'll also get a wealth of training.

Finally, adjust the pricing on your list periodically, to make sure your pricing stays on target.

Make a few different Rehab Price Estimators depending on what type of properties you're walking through. Obviously a rental level rehab will cost less than a property you are selling to a first time home buyer. And that rehab will be far cheaper than a luxury home rehab.

114

Chapter 8: Making Offers

Getting Motivated Sellers
To Say "Yes!"

Making Offers—Getting Motivated Sellers to Say "Yes!"

Now you've identified some potential properties, had the Realtor give you comps to figure out the ARV, and walked trough them to estimate repair costs. You've narrowed your list down to a few properties that you want to make an offer on. Hold on, though. There's an art to making an offer. Let me show you.

First, you want to make it a cash offer. There's a reason why they say "Cash Is King." Put yourself in the seller's shoes: suppose you were selling a house and one guy's got a really complicated list of conditions attached to his offer, like whether or not he can get financing, and that the house must pass inspection, and a few other things. And then there's another guy who has cash in hand and his deal is simple. Whose offer will you take?

You got it. Cash talks and everything else walks. Offering cash will usually get you a better deal. Getting financing is a hassle, even when you're the seller. Most sellers will take less if they can get a good, 100% guaranteed deal for cash, because they know they can count on that deal coming through. A guaranteed Closing is very important to someone who must sell that property so they can move, or buy a new house, or just get out of a bad financial situation.

Cash means your financing is already lined up and secure and there won't be hassles. That's why cash offers are accepted more often. This saves you time and energy because you spend less time making offers that aren't accepted.

However, there will be times your offer won't be accepted. It happens. What do you do then? Well, don't let your emotions get in the way—just realize it's nothing to get mad or upset about. Look for counter-offers. The seller may come

117

back with an offer a few thousand higher than what you offered. If it's a reasonable offer, meaning it's still less than or equal to your MAO (Maximum Acceptable Offer), go with it.

Sometimes, though, you do need to know when to just plain walk away. If you run into a seller whose ego's wrapped up in the price of that property and he or she just won't come down to a reasonable number, walk away. You'd be surprised how many times those people will call you back a day, a week, even a few months later after they've had time to think about it.

You'll also run into sellers who just want to argue back and forth and fight over every detail. If it's a draining power struggle, walk.

How Much To Offer

We decide what we'll pay for a property using a very simple formula. There's no fancy software you'll need, no algebraic equation, and certainly no need for one of those scientific calculators. With just a bit of practice, you'll be able to figure out what to pay for a property *in your head!*

Since this formula is highly reliable, we tend not to deviate from it, much if ever. While we didn't invent this formula, investors have been using it literally for five decades. The first place I ever saw this formula was in a book, long out of print, by an investor named Jimmy Napier. Then I saw it again when Ron LeGrand taught it in his *Quick Turn Real Estate* book. I mean no disrespect, because both of these men are Real Estate geniuses. They probably have over 60 years Real Estate experience combined. Both these guys are the real deal. I've been using this formula successfully myself since I got started in Real Estate, too. So, we have lots of proof this formula works regardless of the market you're in, or your geographical location, or the current market conditions, so why reinvent the wheel. Let's just use what works.

We'll use this simple formula to determine our **Maximum Allowable Offer**, known as the MAO (pronounced "mayo") Formula. MAO is important because when you go to make an offer, you need to know how much to offer *and* how much is too much. Your Maximum Allowable Offer, or MAO is simply the amount of money you can pay for a property without taking a dime out of your own pocket. Every penny you pay *above* MAO is a penny from your pocket. Every penny *below* MAO is **extra profit** in the deal. Don't get confused yet. I'll provide you with a few simple examples so you can really understand.

These three simple components determine the MAO.

- **After Repair Value (ARV)**
- **Costs**
- **Repairs**

You learned in the previous chapter how to determine the ARV. So now, let's take a look at what our costs will be. First, we decide our profit. This is a radically different way of thinking than most people are used to. For many Real Estate investors, the thought process goes like this:

"After the Realtor, the Appraiser, and the Contractor are paid, and all the other bills are paid — if there's any money left over, I'll make a profit. Boy, I sure hope there's money left over!" Folks, I'm here to tell you **hope is not a strategy!** I want to know exactly how much money I'll be making before I decide to make an offer. That's the purpose of MAO.

So the first cost to consider is our profit, or the amount of *equity* we want to have in the property. This will generally run about 20 to 25%. You'll want to plan ahead for when the rehab work is complete and you go to refinance the property so you can pay your original funding source back.

Most lenders will give you a loan that represents 75-to-80% Loan-to-Value (LTV) financing. For the sake of simplicity we assume that the bank will be giving us 80% LTV for our examples. Check with your banker to find out what Loan-to-Value ratio they will be using.

To clarify further, if you buy a property with, say, an ARV of $150,000, rehab it, and then go get financing on it, the bank will give you an 80% LTV mortgage or loan on that property for $120,000. The remaining $30,000 is your equity in the property.

Suppose you decide to sell the property instead. Then the equity number will now become your profit number, less your costs to sell the property, like Realtor commissions, transfer taxes and whatever other fees your locality may charge you. That's $30,000, less expenses, that goes in your pocket!

You'll also need to allow for other costs — generally about 10% of ARV that you need to have in cash.

These costs include:

- 3% for Closing costs (Transfer tax, title insurance, appraisal, attorney's fees)

- 3% for holding costs (Taxes, insurance, debt service, utilities, etc. that you have to pay during the months that the house is being rehabbed.)

- 3% for selling costs (Realtor commissions, marketing costs, etc.)

- 1% for the inevitable Murphy's Law (Whatever can go wrong, will go wrong, at the worst possible time.)

Hopefully you've used your Rehab Price Estimator to estimate the costs of rehabbing the house, and then to calculate

MAO. So let's look at some real-world numbers.

Let's say you find a property and you comp it and the ARV comes up as $100,000. You do a walk-through, checking things off on your worksheet, and you estimate that repairs are going to run about $15,000. Your math looks like this:

ARV	**$100,000**
Repairs	$15,000
30% (Costs)	$30,000
MAO	$55,000

Now just because your MAO is $55,000 in the example above doesn't mean you should necessarily offer $55,000! Remember that the "M" stands for "*Maximum*." Give yourself some negotiating room by offering a figure about 10-15% below MAO. In this case, that would be $46,750 to $50,000. Then, if the seller comes back with a counter-offer of $53,000 or less, take it. People expect to haggle. You know it, I know it. Everyone knows it. It's the Haggle-Factor and we might as well plan for it!

Just one caveat. You may not be able to get away with this in a hot market. By "hot," I mean a seller's market. In that case, your profit margin may be thinner and you'll have to rely on more volume — meaning more deals.

Now let me sum up our current discussion for you with a very, very simple equation:

ARV — (30%) — Repairs = MAO

It just doesn't get any more complex than that. Let's look at a few examples. A three bedroom, one bath rental house has an ARV of $74,000. We decide to hold the property and rent it out for $900. Using our Rehab Price Estimator we determine it needs about $11,000 worth of work. What is the MAO?

ARV	$74,000
Costs (30%)	$22,200
Repairs	$11,000
MAO	$40,800

Remember how we were taught to check our math in school? Start from your result and add backwards to see if your total is correct. MAO, plus repairs, plus our costs of the transaction—Closing, holding and selling costs, and Murphy's Law—leaves us with a profit or equity of 20%. Do it like this:

ARV	$79,000
Purchase Price	$40,800
Rehab	$11,000
Rehab and Realtor Holding	$7,400
Profit ($79,000-$11,000-$7,400)	**$14800**

> NOTE: *If your bank will only loan at 75% LTV you'll need to add another 5% to your costs for properties you decide to rent out for cashflow.*

Real Estate Sales Agreements

Now that you know how much money to offer, I'm going to walk you through the rest of the deal. For your offer to be legal and binding, it MUST be in writing. It's OK to go back and forth with the seller haggling with verbal offers, but when you settle on a figure, in order for your offer to be accepted and lead to a Closing it has to be in writing.

I recommend keeping things as simple as possible, even in Real Estate. The world is already a complicated enough place, why make it worse? So go with a one-page offer and then, once the terms and price are settled, formalize the agreement using the standard Realtor's Agreement of Sale for your state.

Where I live, that's the Pennsylvania Association of Realtors. You have a board in your state—just Google the name of your state and "Realtor board" and it will pop up.

If you're dealing with a Realtor who's selling the property for the owner, be aware Realtors have a code of ethics they are bound by—including that they must present all written offers and counter-offers in a timely manner. See why it's so important to have a *written* offer? Nothing counts in Real Estate unless it's in writing. Another reason to use a written agreement is so the Realtor can keep the seller up to date on the status of the transaction.

When you write up your offer letter, there are a few key things you'll want to include. Make sure every single clause you want is included in that contract. If the seller promised you he was leaving the appliances in the property, record that in a clause. You might even want to record the serial numbers so they don't pull a fast one and replace them with cheaper ones.

You'll also want to use your name or company name with "and/or assigns" so that you can sell that offer if you find a buyer. Yes, it happens—sometimes you find a buyer for a property before you've even bought it yourself, so you flip the contract. That's called wholesaling a deal, and we'll discuss that later in the section of this book on **Exit Strategies.**

A "weasel clause" is also a must, in case you find something seriously wrong with the property, your Contractor's rehab price doesn't jive with yours, or it turns out that the title for the property has issues and they can't sell you the property. You don't want to have to go through with the deal if something like that happens.

And never—*and I mean NEVER*—make an offer if you don't intend to follow through. Your offer is a legally binding contract to buy that property. If you get greedy and put out five offers at the same time and against all the odds every single one of them is accepted, guess what? You're going to buy five houses, or you're going to be wholesaling a few! So don't put out more offers at any one time than it makes sense to follow through on.

You'll also want to put a deadline into that offer, so that you can control just how many active offers you have out there at any given time. When your offer is accepted, a copy of the sales agreement will be sent to a Closing agent of your choice. This means you need to have a Closing agent in your network, so it's a good idea to scout around for one.

To give you an idea of what a one-page offer letter should look like, I've included a sample on the next page. Notice I give them 72 hours to accept it, and I've got some conditions. If the title has problems, or if they fail to give me a statement disclosing all known defects, or if they don't agree to close when I want to close, the offer is invalid.

Note also I've reserved for myself the right to assign this offer to anyone I like. That means that I have the right to wholesale the contract or purchase the property in another company name. For example, if I've offered to buy the property for $50,000 and an investor friend of mine wants to buy my contract for $56,000, I can assign it to him. Also listed is the purchase price and the deadline—the offer, of course, has a specific date on it.

It's a nice short-and-sweet offer. Feel free to copy it and tailor it for your own needs. Each state has its own promulgated Real Estate agreement, and they are available through your state Real Estate board. Contact a local Realtor and they will provide you one for free. You can also go online to your state's Real Estate board and download one.

This is what my typical One-Page Offer looks like. You can download a blank copy for your own customization and use from my website, **www.livetherealestatelifestyle.com/Resources.**

Offer to Purchase Real Property

BE IT KNOWN that the undersigned, Johnny Buyer and/or his assigns, hereinafter called "Buyer," offers to purchase from Eddy Seller, hereinafter called "Seller," the real property known as:

123 South Main Street
Philadelphia, PA 19102

Having Tax ID Number **43-566700-27** in the County of Philadelphia, State of Pennsylvania.

The offer amount for this property is **$117,365** conditioned on the following terms:

1. The property is to be sold free and clear of any and all encumbrances, with clear and marketable title, with full possession to be given on the date of Closing.

2. Seller is to provide a valid Certificate of Occupancy on or before Closing.

3. Closing shall be held on or before **August 23, 2007,** and be extended as necessary to complete all required paperwork.

4. Buyer understands that he is buying this property "AS-IS." Seller is responsible to maintain the property in its current condition until Closing at his own expense.

5. This offer is contingent upon Buyer's acceptance and approval of a General Contractor's quote for repairs of the subject property within **7 days** of the signing of this Agreement.

6. This offer is contingent upon Buyer's acceptance and approval of an Appraisal satisfactory to Buyer within **15 days** of the signing of this Agreement.

7. The parties agree to execute a Standard Purchase and Sales Contract on these terms within **3 days** of the signing of this Agreement.

8. The date of this offer is **July 23, 2007.** This offer expires in 72 hours. Deposit amount with this offer is $500. The balance of the offer price will be paid at Closing.

Buyer _____   Seller _____

Buyer's Agent _____ Phone _____ Seller's Agent _____ Phone _____

Homework: By now, if you've been doing your homework, we've got a lot of the legwork done and we should be ready to submit our first offers together. Congratulations if you are this far along. Now's when it starts to get fun!

First, get your blank Offer to Purchase Real Property form from the Real Estate Lifestyle website **www.livetherealestatelifestyle. com/Resources.** Explain to your Realtor you'll be using this form to save both of you a whole lot of wasted time and effort. Explain that the reason you use a one page document first is to get the ball rolling quickly. To submit 15 full offers each week at up to 25 pages per offer is insanity. You can fill out 15 pages a week and do full offers on the ones where you get counter-offers or the deal is accepted. Now that you have his buy-in, you can proceed. If your Realtor insists on doing a full Agreement of Sale, let him do it for a week or two. He'll quickly find out you're serious and he'll also quickly grow tired of cranking out a few hundred pages of contracts each week!

Submit your first offers using the MAO Formula. Don't deviate from the formula. If your offers are not getting any feedback at all, first check to see if you have not underestimated the After Repair Value, and then make sure you are not over budgeting the cost of repairs. These are the two most common mistakes people make in getting started with their offers. Avoid the temptation to "pad" the numbers. This is merely a symptom of FEAR! Remember, no one can ever MAKE you close on a property and if you act in accordance with the timelines in your offer your deposit is not at risk either. So, relax, breathe and make some offers! You'll soon be hearing "Yes!" and it'll be time to start Closing on properties and making some money!

Chapter 9: Closing the Deal

They Said "Yes!"
Now What Do I Do?

Closing the Deal—They Said "Yes!" Now What Do I Do?

This is my favorite telephone call to receive. I get it all the time from my students and it still excites me. This is when you hear your first, "Yes!" from a Seller. It's that fateful moment when your Realtor calls you to tell you the "good news," you've got your first deal under contract, and you promptly forget everything you've learned about Real Estate investing, so far. That's OK! This is a major milestone for you and it will be emotional. Take a few minutes to celebrate with your friends and family. The Real Estate Lifestyle is about to become real for you! Don't worry. I'll be right here waiting to show you your next steps.

Now that you've made some offers and a seller has accepted one, you need to close the deal, to get to the point where you can use an exit strategy to make money. So, what's a Closing? A Closing is when you legally buy the property — after you close, you own it. Closings are important and you need to make sure you've got your I's dotted and your T's crossed.

The best way to make sure you have everything done right is to find yourself a good Closing attorney or title company. I know, I know…they cost money. But, trust me, though, screwing up a Closing can cost you a whole lot more. It's one of those "you can pay me now or you can pay me much more later" type of things.

You've probably heard of Closing costs, right? These are the expenses you need to pay in order to close the deal. A lot of the usual costs you see in a Closing are on account of the mortgage company, so when you buy the property with investor cash, you don't have many of those costs. The biggest expense you pay when you use a mortgage loan to buy property is the loan origination fee, which is 1% or more of the loan amount.

Mortgage companies make you pay that loan origination fee at Closing to make sure they get some profit out of the deal in case you turn right around the very next day and pay off the mortgage loan (hey, it happens), which means they don't earn any interest on a loan they've spent time setting up. And believe me, mortgage companies are in business to make money.

Now, even when you buy with all cash, you do still have to pay for recording the deed at the county, title insurance, and if you've used a Realtor, you have to pay their percentage.

Just to make sure you understand what's going on, the down payment is not part of the Closing costs. Closing costs come from a variety of sources for several purposes, and tend to be one-time expenses. You want to try to minimize them as much as possible, or get the seller to pay them, as to conserve your cash. These are also known as *settlement costs*.

If you ever do have to use a mortgage loan, one thing your loan officer will do for you fairly quickly after you talk to them about your deal is provide you with a *Good Faith Estimate of Closing Costs*. This is their version of up-front pricing, and it's a good guide to let you know what you're in for as far with Closing costs, in case the Seller isn't paying all of them.

Title Companies and Real Estate Attorneys

Why is it important to always use a title company or an attorney to check the title to the property before you buy it? Well I don't know about you, but I don't like nasty surprises. What if you made a seller an offer, he accepted it, you closed on the property, and then after the property and everything related to it was yours, you found out a Contractor had filed a lien against the property five years ago because he'd never been paid for work he did on the property?

It happens. And it happens for large amounts of money, too. When you buy a property with a mortgage, they require you to use a title company. With cash, you don't have to, but you'd be very foolish not to.

What does the title company do? They search the records on the deed to that property and find anything and everything that might be a problem such as liens, which are someone's money claim against the property. They also find out the really basic stuff, like does that seller actually own the property he's selling to you? You'd be surprised, but people do try to sell property they don't legally own—most commonly in a divorce situation.

The title company will also find out about are any "clouds" on a title, which means its ownership may be unclear. You don't want a clouded title—you want a free and clear title. We also call this "marketable title," which means we could go ahead and sell the property again the very next day.

That title company is your legal representation, so make sure you use a title company or a settlement company for **all** of your Closings. Using a title company also keeps your costs low because it saves you having to pay an attorney to handle the Closing. In some states, like New York, using an attorney is required, so you'll have to account for any extra fees in your numbers. For the rest of us, title companies have attorneys on staff, and they know what to look for.

But what happens if the title company screws up, and they fail to catch a mistake that costs you thousands of bucks? If you've bought title insurance, you've got nothing to worry about. In that case, the title company eats the loss. You can probably guess what this means, but just to be clear: **never**

purchase a property without title insurance. Title insurance assures you that you have clear title to that property after you buy it.

What You Need To Know About Property Insurance

Another MUST for responsible investors is to have insurance on your property, even if you plan to flip it the very next day to a buyer. Insurance isn't something you can put off or do at the last minute, since it will take your insurance company time to get out there and assess the place to give you an amount to pay.

That can take some time, so my suggestion is you contact your insurance agent right after a seller accepts your offer, and start the insurance process.

What you want is to have the insurance go into effect immediately upon Closing, so there's no gap whatsoever where you own the property, but it isn't insured. Think about how ticked off you'd be if you closed on the property, then went to check on your way home, and found it had burned to the ground and the arson investigator says the fire started an hour after you closed on it. If that were to happen, you would lose most of your investment and if you had borrowed money behind you, you'd be up a creek! So, always, always, always have your properties insured from the very minute you close on them.

What kind of insurance do you want to get? Well, there are several types:

- **Actual Cash Value insurance (ACV)** is what most agents will try to sell you. It's the cheapest, but be aware it only pays out what the property is worth at that moment in time. The actual definition of ACV is *replacement value minus depreciation.* How does this work? Well, let's say there's a plumbing leak and it ruins the carpet. That carpet cost me $1,000 new, and the average life of that carpet is nine years. If that carpet has been there for five years, it's only got four years left in it. So if my policy was ACV, the insurance payout would be ⁴⁄₉ of $1,000, or $444.44. *(4/9 x $1000 = $444.44)*

The problem with ACV insurance is, where are you going to find 5-year-old carpet to buy? Unless you buy used stuff — and why would you do that? — you're going to be in the hole for the difference between the amount this ACV formula allows for and the amount you need to pay to actually replace the carpet and make it new again.

- **Replacement Value insurance** costs more, but it's more realistic since it pays the actual cost to replace the carpet or whatever you're claiming. In this case, if you bought that carpet five years ago for $1,000, and now with inflation it costs $1,150 to get that same grade carpet, they'll pay you that amount. Replacement value is vital for the structure, particularly if the property is old.

Don't fall into the trap of thinking you'll insure your properties, and then let insurance pick up the tab for anything that goes wrong. You need to understand how insurance companies work. They play the percentages with very complicated computer models, and what those models tell them is someone who makes three or more claims in a year is likely to keep on making lots of claims. So when those people's policies expire, the insurance companies drop them by sending out a non-renewal notice.

And then, when you try to get another company, they'll pull your claim history, and they probably won't want to underwrite you, either. Believe it or not, the insurance business isn't that big, and the agents in your area talk to each other, and share information about you via computer systems. You don't want to get a reputation as someone who makes lots of claims, because eventually it will catch up with you. Then no one will write your policies.

OK, I know, this sounds like I'm speaking out of both sides of my mouth:

"Buy insurance."

"But don't make claims."

That's not quite what I mean. What I mean is that you should be very careful in making claims, and only make them when you REALLY need to, for very large expenses you just don't have the cash to handle.

As far as deductibles are concerned, you'll be offered a broad range of them. If you've had car insurance, you know how this works: you can take a very low deductible, but it'll cost you. Or, you can take the very highest deductible, pay for most things out of your own pocket, and pay a low insurance premium.

I highly recommend your choosing a very high deductible- you'll save money by getting the least-expensive policy. You'll also keep yourself out of trouble, since you won't be tempted to make claims for small stuff, or do shabby rehab work since the insurance company will handle your mistakes.

Getting Utilities

You'll need to make arrangements to put the utilities in your name at Closing. This includes electric, gas, water, waste-water, and maybe garbage pick-up depending where you buy property. Also, make sure you put those phone numbers on a

Vendor Contact List you will give to your Property Manager. These will be vendors you want them to use, such as a designated plumber, electrician, handyman, painter, etc.

And if your area allows it, put the put the utilities in your company name, not your personal name.

About Closing Costs

You know the saying, "Money makes the world go round." Well, now it's time to talk about Closing costs and you should always remember there are legitimate and not so legitimate Closing costs. It's up to you to educate yourself and make sure you are not being taken advantage of.

With that said, let's look at the different Closing costs. If you're using a bank for a mortgage, your Closing costs will fall into four categories:

1. Points, Discount Points, or Loan Origination Fees— Each point represents 1% of the total loan amount. Points are essentially fees you are paying up front in exchange for a lower interest rate over time. Often you can get a better interest rate by paying a point or two, but bear in mind, cash is king. However, if you can get the seller to pay the points for you, then try to get as much out of it as you can, since that will simply lower the interest rate you have to pay over time, improving the long-term cashflow in the deal.

2. "Hard" Closing Costs—These are fixed transaction fees charged by the service providers involved in the transaction. These include the Closing attorney's fee; the title search (to make sure there's no cloud on the title); survey, termite inspection, appraisal, credit report, document preparation, courier fees, tax service, title insurance, and inspections.

These fees may not be quite as *"hard"* as the lender makes them out to be, so ask if you can set up these services yourself. Don't be afraid to challenge anyone on any fees that look suspicious to you. Although the industry has been getting much better recently, they are notorious for throwing in extra fees for unnecessary items, just to boost their bottom line. Remember, the worst thing anyone can do is say "no" if you ask them to remove the charge. The bank will still give you the loan, and the seller will still sell you the house. Let me give you an example of what I call a "junk fee." Among Realtors there's the notorious "Broker's Service Fee," an absolutely ridiculous charge for service, since the Realtors are all being paid a commission on your transaction. So, any work they do should be fully covered under the compensation they receive from their commission. All things are negotiable, and no one can ever make you close on a property.

3. Municipal and Government Charges—These are taxes and fees required by the city, county, or state. Such items include fees to record the deed in county records, transfer tax, tax stamps, and any applicable sales taxes. These items will be prorated on your Closing statement. If you've already paid your trash pickup for the entire year it will be a credit to you at Closing. Also, most states and counties charge a transfer tax, or a flat tax based on the total amount of the sale. The can be from 1% to 6% and depends on your specific locality. Any Realtor can tell you exactly how much the transfer tax is in your area.

4. Prepaid Items—This category includes payments at Closing as the responsibility of the property owner that will come due again in the future, such as pro-rated taxes, homeowner's insurance, flood insurance if needed,

Private Mortgage Insurance, known as PMI (if you can't get out of it), and interim types of insurance, like vacant property insurance.

Closing costs on an all-cash deal will run you about 2-3%. If you use financing, you're looking at about 3-4%. Then there's the Realtor's fee, which is usually about 3%.

Another terrific advantage of buying with cash is you can close quicker. You can probably offer the seller a Closing within two weeks if you have your Closing service or attorney all lined up and your investor cash ready. Sellers love that, since they need the cash ASAP. Many times I got a property for less than someone else had offered, simply because I could close on the property faster than someone needing traditional financing.

So what are you looking at to close a deal, cost-wise? Let's look at a deal I did in the Frankford area of Philadelphia. I purchased a fixer-upper house for $32,000. It cost me $640 in Closing costs to buy it since the seller paid my transfer tax (2% of $32,000), $2,300 to rehab it, and then I sold it for $45,000. At the second Closing, when I sold it, I paid $900 in Closing costs, since the buyer paid my half of the transfer tax (2% of $45,000) and $1,350 to the Realtor who sold it (3% of $45,000). So my net profit was $7,810.

How this deal played out:

Costs: $32,000 + $640 + $2,300 + $900 + $1,350 = $37,190

Selling price: $45,000

Profit: $45,000 − $37,190 = $7,810

Purchase price	**$32,000**
Closing costs to buy	$640
Rehab costs	$2,300
Closing costs to sell	$900
Realtor costs	$1,350
Sale price	$45,000
Profit	**$7,810**

Anatomy and Timeline of a Real Estate Deal

Before the Closing, a handful of things need to be done. I advise that when you're doing your first few deals you complete the majority of steps on your own. This will give you the opportunity to learn and understand ALL the mechanics of the deal. This is an important step in building your foundation of tactical Real Estate knowledge.

Later, once you are working toward doing Real Estate as a Lifestyle Business, and your personal knowledge base is built, we'll let other people do this work for free. That's right! I said Free. Most Realtors will volunteer to do the work of getting your deals to the Closing table for you, and there are several reasons why.

First, they want to make sure the deal closes! That's the

only way they make their commission. Second, many Real Estate offices offer these services in-house, meaning their broker already has a Title Company, a Mortgage Company and insurance services their firm's associated with. These are called *value-added* services, which I have nothing against, but essentially these are money-making opportunities for other people—and you'll eventually be footing the bill.

So if you understand from firsthand experience what needs to be done during the transaction, your likelihood of being taken advantage of is greatly reduced.

Now that we have all the warnings out of the way, the process is really pretty simple and you'll be stunned at how smoothly things go. When you get finished your first Closing and realize your head hasn't exploded, you'll be really happy you got started in Real Estate investing, and NOW, *you are a Real Estate investor, too!*

So let's take a look at the steps required one by one so you can see how easy it really is:

Day 1 Submit your "Offer To Purchase Real Property." Remember, your offer expires in 72 hours—so that's the first three days.

Day 4 Latest date for "Offer to Purchase Real Property" to be valid. You must receive a SIGNED copy. Remember, a verbal agreement IS NOT a valid Agreement. If you've heard nothing on your offer, it's now time to call your Realtor and ask them to follow up. If your offer has been accepted proceed to **Days 4–9.**

Days 4–9 Double-check your numbers and get your General Contractor through the property to double check your rehab costs. Compare his price to your Rehab Price Estimator and handle any discrepancies. Now get his proposal in writing!

Days 4–9 If you are getting an appraisal done on the property, make sure that it is ordered. I advise going to the scheduled appraisal so you can meet the Property Appraiser and hear his opinion first hand. Bring any comps you believe are similar to the property you are buying. It's always an educational experience to talk to Appraisers about current market conditions. They may not be investors; however, they work closely with the banks and know what they are thinking about Real Estate in your investing area at the moment.

Days 4–9 Have your Realtor check with the Seller's side to see if the Certificate of Occupancy was ordered. If not, have them do so immediately.

Day 9 Submit a formal State Sponsored "Standard Agreement of Sale" form on the same terms—and your deposit money.

Days 9–14 Receive signed "Standard Agreement of Sale" form and check to make sure no changes have been made.

Day 14 Receive the written appraisal and double check your numbers now that you are dealing with facts and not estimates. If things don't jive, NOW is the time to back out of the deal and get your deposit back. If you need to back out after today, for any reason, you'll forfeit your deposit. If everything looks good, proceed with confidence!

Day 15 Call your Title Company and let them know you will be faxing the signed Agreement of Sale. Supply them with the following in writing:

- The Closing date and time
- Address of the property
- SSN or EIN of the Seller and Buyer
- Your Articles of Incorporation

Day 16 Call your Title Company and confirm they have received your information and ask if they need anything else. Confirm the Closing date.

Day 16 Call your General Contractor. Ask him to do the following in the next 3 days:

- Visit the property again
- Put the final work list together
- Provide you with the work schedule, including completion date

Day 16 If you'll be doing a cleanout (furniture, debris, etc.) call the Cleanout Company and ask them to do the following in the next 3 days:

- Visit the property
- Put the work list and price together
- Provide you the work schedule, including completion date

Day 17 Call the Utility Companies (Gas, Electric and Water) to transfer the utility services to your company name effective on the date of settlement. The title company will get the final meter readings for Closing.

Day 19 Call the Property Insurance Company and arrange coverage to begin for your Closing date.

Day 25 Call the Title Company again to verify the Closing date is still as planned and all required paperwork is in their office. Ask them to FAX or email you a copy of the preliminary HUD-1 Settlement Sheet. Review it to be sure there are no junk fees.

Closing Arrive at Closing a few minutes early. Bring the following with you:

- Certified Check made out to the Title Company or Attorney's office

- Articles or Organization for your company
- LLC Operating Agreement or Corporation Shareholder Agreement
- Proof of Insurance
- Photo Identification

At Closing: Be sure to leave with a "marked up" copy of the Title, the deed and the keys.

Day 30 Call the Bank to Refinance the property and schedule the appraisal.

What to Bring to Closing, What to Leave With

While we've already discussed preparations, it bears repeating. Bring the following documents to Closing with you:

1. Driver's License — to prove your identity.

2. Operating Agreement of your corporation — to satisfy legal requirements.

3. Articles of Organization- to satisfy entity ownership requirements.

4. Certified Check — to pay for the property, Closing costs, and any fees. You'll be given an exact amount by the title company.

When you leave the Closing, make sure you have:

1. A marked-up copy of the title (Leave the title "open" for cheaper and faster refinancing).

2. A copy of the deed.

- The Title and Deed should be in your Corporate name.

- All parties associated with the property purchased should be listed on the deed.

3. The keys! You'd be surprised how many times people leave Closing without the keys to the property. It's an exciting time and the keys are easy to forget. Keys are much harder to get after the Closing is over.

Homework: Let's prepare for your first Closing. Go to the companion website for this book at **www.livetherealestatelife style.com/Resources** and download my **Successful Closing Check List.** Print it out and put it in a prominent place where you will see it on a daily basis. Remember, repetition is the mother of skill. The more often you see the checklist, the more often you read and review it, the more likely you are to not miss any important steps. But don't stress out here. Between your Realtor and your Settlement Agent or Closing Company, most things will run very smoothly. You only need to oversee this process the first few times, or if you're working with a new Realtor. Soon, this process will be on auto-pilot because you'll be living your own Real Estate Lifestyle!

Chapter 10: Fixing Up Properties

*Quick and Effective Rehabbing
for Maximum Profits*

Fixing Up Properties - Quick and Effective Rehabbing for Maximum Profits

A
t this stage of the game, you are now the owner of the property. It's now time to get it fixed up so you can sell it or get a tenant in there and have it refinanced. There's a whole strategy to fixing up properties. Ideally, you picked this property to buy because it didn't have any major structural damage costing you a lot more to fix than you'd ever make on selling it, or renting it out. But you probably have a lot of cosmetic repairs and slightly deeper stuff to fix, like maybe a busted stove or a hole in the wall, or a toilet or hot water heater that needs to be replaced.

Your basic strategy should be:

1. Fix anything that requires repair to bring it up to local building and safety codes.

2. Fix anything broken, such as light fixtures, doorknobs, the stove, or windows that won't open or shut.

3. Fix any problem areas, like broken doors and holes in walls and ceilings.

4. Give the place the maximum amount of Curb Appeal for the money. You're looking to increase the **perceived** value.

It should be pretty obvious what you need to fix, but what about Curb Appeal? Where should you spend money so you get the most for your rehab dollars? After all, if you install a Jacuzzi tub in the front yard, what are the odds it'll get you the return on investment that you're looking for? Better yet, what are the odds it'll still be in the front yard in the morning? I say that in jest, but we need to consider what items will best improve the property, without going crazy as though we were going to live there.

First, you need to understand this: even the most savvy buyers can be swayed into paying more for a place if it sparkles and shines. Nothing's as sweet as the smell of fresh paint and the crisp look of new carpet. Or the look of ceiling fans and mini-blinds — not at all expensive. So you should plan to always repaint the inside and outside and replace the carpet. You'll also want to take a close look at the trim-work — baseboards and door frames — repair, replace, and repaint as necessary. You must make sure the place is absolutely as neat and clean as you can make it.

When you choose paint and carpet colors, keep them neutral. For paint, use white, off-white, or my favorite, a very light beige. Carpet should be beige, or light brown. When you stick with neutral colors, your paint and carpet won't clash with 90% of people's furniture or furnishings. This is not the time to get creative and use wild colors. Let the new resident do that.

Give the bathrooms and kitchen extra attention, since these areas give you the biggest payoff for the renovation money you invest in them. If you need to replace the fixtures and appliances, don't go for the absolute cheapest ones, unless the property is very low income housing. Instead, go one small step up into slightly nicer fixtures. This won't cost you much more money, but it will say "quality" and "maintenance-free" to prospective buyers and renters.

If you think you might want to keep the property for a rental, avoid making any improvements which are risky to anyone's safety or constitute what lawyers and insurance companies call an "**attractive nuisance**."

An attractive nuisance is something irresistible to immature, irresponsible people, yet dangerous to them. The classic example is a swimming pool. Now, I personally love swimming pools, but you really don't want one in your rental house, or duplex, or quad for the simple reason they can be liability nightmares.

And it's not just the potential for drowning that dooms swimming pools. Drunken party guests are notorious for diving head first into the shallow end and breaking their necks or getting a traumatic, permanent head injury. The medical costs involved are huge and can be an insurance catastrophe. The same goes for hot tubs.

You may also want to avoid installing basketball nets in or near the driveway, since children playing there often chase balls out into the street, and you know what can happen on a busy street.

From an aesthetic perspective, I would also avoid installing any high-grade flooring such as Berber carpet or Pergo hardwoods, even in middle-class properties. But don't go too cheap. Use medium-grade carpet with a good pad—it doesn't look cheap, yet it isn't too expensive. Good padding—the layer that goes under the carpet—is far more important for comfort and durability than the actual carpet.

For rental properties, you have to consider the worst-case scenario for wear and tear on a property—sloppy tenants with kids and pets. If you have any combination of those three, I guarantee you that carpet will get abused. Expect to replace it every three to four years, and expect to paint the place that often, too. For this reason, look into a pet-resistant carpet, with Scotch Guard™ protection or its equivalent.

And watch out for over-improving a property. What do I mean by that? Well, you may have heard the properties that appreciate the most in value are valued at or around the median price for the neighborhood. So it's a good idea to buy something slightly under median—since it will be inexpensive—and use cost-effective improvements to bring it up to the median level.

According to the Law of Diminishing Returns, once you've passed the median value for the neighborhood, making additional improvements starts to gain you less and less in equity appreciation. Careful, you'll never get your money out of a house that's way too grand for its neighborhood.

A common mistake Real Estate investors make is buying a lower-income property and then fixing it up too nicely, as if they, themselves, are going to live there. Sure, it's great to take pride in your properties. I do, and you should, too, but you can't get emotionally wrapped up in them. You aren't going to live there. Fixtures and such are simply investments and investments need to pay off.

The Top 7 Items to Improve

Since I brought up return on investment for your rehab dollars, let me tell you the top seven items with the biggest return for your rehab dollar. If you focus on these, you'll always be pleased with your return and your buyers and renters will always be pleased with their new property.

1. **Paint**—There's nothing like a fresh coat of interior and exterior paint to spruce up a place. Remember, always use neutral colors.

2. **Carpet**—New carpet really shows off a place. Don't waste money on anything better than medium-grade, and in a very low-income place, you may want to go with a cheaper grade. Always use a good padding though, as it extends the life of the carpet, and it feels good to walk on.

3. **Landscaping**—This is called "Curb Appeal," since it will make prospective tenants get out of the car when

they pull up to check out a place for rent. Cut the grass frequently, trim the bushes, cut back trees so they don't block windows, edge the grass around walkways and the driveway, and plant lots of colorful flowers. Keeping walkways and driveways swept works wonders, too—it gives a property that neat look.

4. **New appliances**—If the stove, dishwasher, and refrigerator are visibly old, replace them. Don't go too cheap, since cheap appliances break and must be replaced frequently. Go medium-grade.

5. **New kitchen and bath cabinets**—Again, if the current ones look old and very worn, consider replacing them with medium-grade cabinets.

6. **New vanities**—Nice, new countertops and sinks can really add to perceived value, so if the old ones are cracked, chipped, and stained, replace them.

7. **Ceiling Fans**—I've saved the best for last. This one item has made me more money than all the others combined, but it's almost always overlooked by my competitors. I use a larger ceiling fan with three lights in the main living room, and smaller ceiling fans in each bedroom, this time with one light. There are two reasons for this. First, it gives the impression the property will be cooler in the summer. Next, in a darker property, or for winter showings when the sun goes down early, the lights work wonders in brightening up the place. Use dimmer switches on all ceiling fans with lights.

Working with Contractors

I once met a very honest Contractor whose motto was, "I might not be old, but I'm slow." All kidding aside, though, you need to start building up your "go-to" list of responsible Contractors and handymen who will do a first-rate job at a fair price, and who can be counted on to show up.

How do you find these people? The best way is through referrals. Use Service Provider lists Realtors have. Go to Real Estate investment club meetings. Or visit your local building supplies store and ask around.

When you call the Contractor ask for references, including names and phone numbers, and then call and check them. Also ask the Contractor to show you proof of insurance (Liability and Worker's Compensation Insurance) so you know if he or one of his workers gets hurt on the job, it's covered.

While there may be unscrupulous Contractors out there. There are also really good, honest ones. When you find a decent one, treat him fairly and cultivate a good working relationship with him. That will save you having to hunt for another Contractor and give you peace of mind.

Here are a few measures you'll want to take to protect yourself from unscrupulous Contractors:

- Get three competitive estimates before you award your business to any Contractor.

- **NEVER** pay by the hour—They will take their sweet time if you do that.

- **NEVER** pay up front—Some Contractors will use your money to finish someone else's job and then complain they need more money to get started on yours.

  –Provide low draws—Ask for an estimate of materials

and front them the money for them. Every now and then, go to Home Depot or wherever and check prices yourself to make sure those estimates are accurate and not inflated.

–Progressive Payments—Make an agreement to pay in stages, with each payment tied to the completion of a phase of work. They don't get the money until that stage is complete.

- Get itemized written estimates—Don't accept ballpark numbers like, "I think we can get this done for about $5,000." Get that dollar amount broken down by materials and labor, and on the labor have them state their hourly rate and estimated man-hours.

  –Include start and completion dates—This is very important. If you don't get this in writing, they can put you off for a more profitable job. You might also want to work in a penalty for being late on completion that docks their pay for every day or week they're late in finishing the project. Good Contractors are hard to find, and once they do get found, they get overbooked. When that happens, the squeaky wheel gets the grease. Be the squeaky wheel.

- Monitor Progress and Quality of Work—I can't stress highly enough how important it is that you stay on top of Contractors and what they're doing. You or someone who works for you should go over to the property either every day or every other day to check on progress and to make sure those Contractors are using quality materials and doing the job right. This also sends an important message that you're watching closely.

- Don't make final payment until <u>ALL</u> work is 100% complete — The reason for this should be obvious, but just in case it's not, once you give them the final payment, they have no real incentive to come back and finish up any little details that aren't done yet. I've made this mistake before and it took me two months of phone tag and tracking the guy down to get something completed.

What to Include in a Contractor's Contract

When you make an agreement with a Contractor to fix up a property or remodel it in some way, you need that agreement in writing. And that's all a contract is, a written agreement. Still, you'll want to make sure you include several key details:

- **Start date** — When the project begins.

- **Estimated completion time** — How long it will take, and on what date will the work be completed.

- **The job must be completed on time and in a quality manner** — Yes, you need this in writing. If you don't have it in writing, they may take their sweet time and if some other high-paying work comes along while they're in the middle of your project, they'll disappear for a long, long time… maybe even forever. You also have to specify workmanship standards or the Contractor could subcontract your work out to the cheapest manual laborer they can find.

- **Sub-standard materials are NOT permitted** — This is where they get you. If you don't specify the grade of materials or fixtures, they WILL use the cheapest thing Home Depot has in stock.

- **Disputes over sub-standard work will be handled**

through arbitration — You want this clause because if you don't have it, and they do poor work and you refuse to pay, they can file a lien against your property or sue you. This clause forces both of you to use a mediator, which is much cheaper than suing.

- **Any damage that occurs during the process of completing the job <u>will</u> be deducted from the bid price** — This is very important. Suppose one of the workers swings a big ladder around and knocks a hole in the wall? This clause means they better get it fixed or it's coming out of their pay.

You can find the actual contract I use with my own Contractors for your own use on my website at **www.livethereal estatelifestyle.com/Resources**. Of course, you should be sure to check with your own attorney to be sure this contract is enforceable in your own state or locality.

How to Assess the Property and Decide What to Fix

Since you're paying cash, you won't have a mortgage company looking over your shoulder, requiring you to hire a property inspector. But the property still needs to be inspected, before you buy it, to see what you need to do to rehab it so you can work up some kind of rehab price estimate.

The truth is, it's not hard to do most of this yourself. If you run into things that could be major problems, depending on your level of expertise with houses, you may want to call in an expert like a plumber, electrician, or HVAC specialist to check it out. But most of it you can estimate on your own. Remember, we only need an *estimate* of the price to do the repairs. We already have a buffer built in to our numbers in

You can find a digital copy of my **Rehab Price Estimator** on the MAO Formula. But before you go walking into houses to estimate repairs you'll want to bring your Property Tool Bag along with you.

Actually, I recommend two basic sets of tools for assessing properties, one on your person and one in your car.

Tools to keep on your person:

- **A D-cell battery Maglite® flashlight** — The big kind you can use as a hammer or club

- **A voice recorder** — To take notes on the spot. You can get these for $25 to $50 at office supply stores.

- **A digital camera** — Downloading photos digitally to your computer is easiest, but any camera will work. Think cheap and rugged.

- **A baseball cap** — With a brim, to keep debris and crud from falling into your hair and eyes when you're in basements.

- **Copies of your Rehab Price Estimator** — To tally up areas that need work.

- **A pen** — One that works.

Tools to keep in your car:

- **Waterless hand cleaner** — Any inexpensive alcohol-based hand sanitizer will do.

- **Spare batteries** — Including 4 D-cells and batteries for your digital camera.

- **Small screwdrivers**– Phillips and flathead.

- **Calculator**

- **Copies of your Agreement to Purchase Real Property** — So you can decide how much to offer and write it up while you're *still at the property*. It's all about making offers!

- **Rubber gloves** — For handling greasy, dirty stuff.

- **Business cards** — A must. Never know when you'll meet someone and want to give them your contact info.

Rehab Price Estimator

You should have already used this tool a few times while doing your homework in **Chapter 6: Finding A Deal**. *I've included my* **Rehab Price Estimator** *on the following page for further discussion. The better you get at using this tool, the quicker and more accurate you'll become at estimating the cost of repairs for your potential deals. Of course, the more accurate you become, the more offers you'll get accepted.*

The Rehab Price Estimator is a list of the usual repairs that I find my General Contractor making over and over again. Since I found that he makes mostly the same repairs again and again, I asked him to give me his pricing for each item. Once I had that information I could simply count the number of things I needed and just multiply across to get a relatively accurate price. For example, most windows in my area cost about $225 a piece, installed. That's the price of the window and the actual installation of the window. Now, not all windows cost $200, for example the window in most bathrooms are rather small and only cost $125, but on average windows cost $200 installed. Remember we're getting an estimate! So feel free to take this sheet to your Contractor so you can get accurate prices for your area.

You can also get your own copy of my new DVD, *HOW TO ESTIMATE REPAIRS LIKE A PRO IN 7 MINUTES OR LESS.* In this professionally shot DVD and Workbook program, I personally walk you through several of my projects, before and after, showing you exactly what work I felt needed to be performed, what the costs were, how I determined the Punch List, and what the completed projects look like. I include a few rental projects, as well as a retail project I sold to a first-time homebuyer for a $50,000 profit! This program provides an excellent first-hand educational experience and it's a perfect addition to your Real Estate investor education and training.

Consider this: How much would you pay to quickly further your goal of becoming a successful Real Estate investor, by getting to tag along with another millionaire Real Estate investor as he determines the nitty-gritty of his trade—what price to pay for a property, what exit strategy to use for the maximum profit potential, and most importantly, to see the deal the way a professional investor sees it? If you're like me, you'd pay a pretty handsome sum—but you won't have to when you buy this DVD program.

Just visit the companion website to this book at **www.livetherealestatelifestyle.com/Resources** and click on the link for **How To Estimate Repairs Like a Pro In 7 Minutes or Less DVD/Workbook Program.** You'll pay only $79 plus shipping and handling for the DVD and Workbook when you use discount code **RELBOOKLOVER1.** I hope you'll take advantage of this excellent resource today, because it's certain to make you your money back again, and again, and again!

Rehab Price Estimator ™

Rental Level Repair Worksheet

Description	Needed	Number	Price	Per	Total
Demo/Debris Removal	Yes/No		$500	Day (3 Men)	
Dumpster	Yes/No		$750	40 Yard	
Roofing Flat - 3 Ply 10 Yr.	Yes/No		$1,500	1500 Sq. Ft Row	
Roofing Coating (Flat Only)	Yes/No		$500	1500 Sq.Ft Row	
Roofing Shingled	Yes/No		$4,000	1500 Sq. Ft. Single	
Siding	Yes/No		$900	Wall 3 Story	
Brick Painting	Yes/No		$1,250	Wall 3 Story	
Stucco	Yes/No		$1,000	Wall 3 Story	
Exterior Paint	Yes/No		$500	Wall 3 Story	
Gutters and Downspouts	Yes/No		$500	House	
Exterior Security Doors	Yes/No		$300	Piece	
Storm Doors	Yes/No		$150	Piece	
Ceiling Fans	Yes/No		$75	Piece	
Miniblinds	Yes/No		$10	Piece	
Windows - Double Hung	Yes/No		$225	Piece	
Windows - Glass Block	Yes/No		$250	Piece	
Drywall - Hung/Taped	Yes/No		$500	Room	
Interior Paint (2 Coats)	Yes/No		$1.25	Sq. Ft.	
Carpet/Flooring	Yes/No		$1.25	Sq. Ft.	
Ceiling Tiles (Drop)	Yes/No		$1.25	Sq. Ft.	
Kitchen (Complete)	Yes/No		$2,500	Piece	
Bathroom (Tub Coat)	Yes/No		$1,000	Piece	
Bathroom (Tub Replaced)	Yes/No		$1,500	Piece	
Electric Service Line (60-150 AMP)	Yes/No		$500	Piece	
Electric Service Breaker Box	Yes/No		$500	Run	
Electric Cabling (Homerun)	Yes/No		$100	Run	
Light Switches/Outlets (est. 40)	Yes/No		$5	Piece	
Plumbing - 4" Main	Yes/No		$475	Piece	
Plumbing - 1" Main	Yes/No		$125	Run	
PVC Sewer Line	Yes/No		$250	6' Section	
Heater - Forced Hot Air (90% Eff)	Yes/No		$2,000	Piece	
Heater - Boiler (90% Eff)	Yes/No		$2,000	Piece	
Hot Water Heater - 30 Gallon	Yes/No		$450	Piece	
Seal Basement/Concrete	Yes/No		$1,000	1500 Sq.Ft Row	
Termite Treatment	Yes/No		$500	1500 Sq.Ft Row	
Rodent/Pest Treatment	Yes/No		$500	1500 Sq.Ft Row	
Miscellaneous (mailbox, doorbell)	Yes/No		$500	1500 Sq.Ft Row	
Other	Yes/No				
Other	Yes/No				
Other	Yes/No				
				Total Repair Estimate:	

Property Address:

Notes:

You can find a digital copy of my **Rehab Price Estimator** on this book's companion website, **www.livetherealestatelife style.com/Resources.** There you will find three different versions: one for Rental property rehab, one for Retail property rehab, and a blank template you can use to completely customize your own list. You can take it to your Contractor (or to a few of them) and ask them to fill in the prices for the most common items you'll need fixed. Remind your Contractor you're looking for an estimate, not the number he'll always have to commit to for the rehab price.

Homework: Now you've made it this far through the Real Estate Lifestyle System, it's time to start putting it all together. One of my Coaches has a saying, "Repetition is the mother of skill"—which I'm sure you'll also discover is true. But remember that fear problem we discussed earlier? Well, here's how we'll handle it. For a while, we'll take a few baby steps. What I mean is, we'll start doing this for real now, but we'll do it in a safe environment where you can't get hurt.

For instance, if you've ever taken a course in the Stock Market— stocks, commodities, or stock options, they're big on **paper trading**. What's paper trading? Picking the stocks, pretending to buy them, writing that down in a notebook or noting it in a spreadsheet, deciding when to sell, and then calculating profits—all on paper. No risk, no money, no losses, no reason to be scared. Well, they have you practice doing that on paper, without using real money, for two months to get the feel of how to do it and get a sense of the Market and how it moves.

Paperless Real Estate: Let's borrow this paperless idea for the next few days and see what kind of results you have. Here's how to do Real Estate paper deals:

    1. Get your listings sent to you by e-mail. Look for the

keywords we discussed earlier. Or you can talk to a Realtor, and collect 20 "possibles."

2. Drive by the properties that make sense—probably about 10 of them.

3. Walk through at least 5 properties. This is not the time to get shy. Six or seven would be even better!

When you do your walk-throughs: Estimate repairs using your Rehab Price Estimator. Remember to keep your emotions in check! So what if it smells, or it's dark or messy… That's potential. Then, write down your questions. Finally, prepare your MAO in writing for all properties you visit.

Now, let me explain why all this is important. If you start doing these things right away, you'll begin to develop a comfort level with your own skills and competence. For even more validation of your skills, take your Rehab Price Estimator to your General Contractor and ask him to verify your numbers with his findings on the same property. If you are close, that's great! If not, ask him to show you what you missed so you can get it right next time.

Tip: When I was getting started in creating my own Real Estate Lifestyle, I paid a Home Inspector about $200 for a half-day of his time. I asked him to walk through vacant houses with me and show me what various problems looked like—termites, cracked sewer lines, etc. It may be a good idea for you to try that, too!

Chapter 11: Getting Paid

The Four Major Exit Strategies

Getting Paid—The Four Major Exit Strategies

Some people say there's only one way to do Real Estate… Well, guess what? They're wrong! While other people KNOW there are literally hundreds of ways to do Real Estate… And they're right! However, all the ways to do Real Estate available to investors are derived from just **four** major exit strategies.

Personally, I'm a firm believer once you understand how the nuts and bolts of a thing works, you can mix and match to get your desired outcome. So here are the four major exit strategies — **wholesaling, retailing, renting and using options.**

If you combine the last three — retailing, renting and options — you get lease options or the rent-to-own exit strategy. You still need to understand all three, but if you understand each exit strategy and you're prepared to use them, you'll do very well as a Real Estate investor.

The same holds true in the Stock Market. Plenty of people go in with the "buy, hold, and pray" mentality. These people can only make money when the Stock Market is trending up. However, they give back all the money they made in the good times when the Stock Market corrects, or goes into a downward cycle.

Since markets always go up *and* down, we need to be able to make money in every cycle. Having multiple exit strategies at your disposal is the only way to make that possible.

So, now you've bought the property and fixed it up, what will you do next? Since this is an investment property, you need to decide how you're going to make money from this property. Ideally, this is a decision you'll want to be making as you are making the decision to buy, but hey…that's why we've been doing this on paper.

Now, let me walk you through each of the four basic exit strategies. The exit strategy you pick will determine your profit structure.

You can:

- **Wholesale the property** — Sell the contract to buy the property.

- **Retail the property** — Sell the actual property.

- **Rent the property out** — Sell the use of the property.

- **Option the property** — Buy or sell the right to buy the property.

Exit Strategy 1: Wholesale the Property

Wholesaling can be a great way to do some quick deals in a short amount of time to build up some cash. This is by far the most useful of all Real Estate investing skills to have. Why? Some people don't make a lot of offers because they don't know what they'll do if they get more than one under contract. As a result, they are very shy about making offers. Not me, though! I have the ability to turn too many properties into CASH! And quickly, too!

Some less-than-scrupulous people, who try to hyper-complicate this wholesaling process, recommend you do "double-closings" and lots of other malarkey. They also charge thousands of dollars to teach you how to do what I'm going to explain in about three pages. They make all this money because people who haven't ever done a wholesale deal really can't believe how easy it is. And because they believe it can't be that easy, they spend thousands of dollars trying to prove themselves right. One "Guru" I know of has a 7 CD series on wholesaling. Each CD is about 30 minutes and two CDs are made up of the Guru reading a wholesaling contract; the 7th CD is a "forms" CD with an 8-page wholesaling contract — absolutely unnecessary — in seven different languages! Promise me you won't be duped into spending big money for someone else to teach you what I'm teaching you right now.

Do we have a deal?

Whew! Okay, now that we've straightened that out, what is wholesaling? As a veteran Real Estate guy I know says, "When you wholesale a property, you're a bargain hunter for bargain hunters."

What this means is you go out and find the fixer-uppers, you talk to the sellers, negotiate the price, and then put the property under contract. Once you've done that, you sell that contract to another investor. The contract is just a piece of paper which gives you the right to buy that property for a certain price within a certain period of time, assuming the property is in reasonable shape. You never actually own the property, and you never have to actually rehab the property. You don't involve your credit, or even any money, except maybe a small deposit you'll get back when you assign the contract.

Many offers you might make would lend themselves to wholesaling possibilities. Say you put out several offers and two are accepted, but you can only handle one at a time–so you might wholesale the other and make some money from it. Maybe you have bad credit, or no ability to obtain cash to buy a property, yet. That's where wholesaling comes in.

Let's get right to it.

The key clause in the contract you sign with the seller is the *right to assign,* which gives you the right to sell that contract to anyone you want. Important point: you're not selling the house — that's what Realtors do– you're just selling a contract.

There's a way you want to word this. When you put your name on the contract, you add: *"And/Or Assigns"* after your name or your company name as the Buyer on the contract. Be sure to strike any language in your state's Agreement of Sale with any restriction on assigning the contract, or requiring the Seller's permission before signing it. Any competent Realtor can show you where this section of the contract is.

When you sell the contract to another investor, you can either use another contract or write directly on the Agreement of Sale, this simple language:

"I, (YOUR NAME), hereby assign this contract and all its obligations, duties and benefits to (BUYER'S NAME) for good and valuable consideration, received on this (DATE)."

Get that contract signed and dated by both of you, and make sure you get paid before the buyer goes off with the Agreement of Sale.

Many new investors get started by wholesaling since it is quick, easy, and hassle-free. It also gives you plenty of rewards during the learning process since you actually are paid when you get a property under contract at a good price. Remember, you don't have to fix anything up because you'll never own the property — you simply own the right to buy it.

How much money can you make wholesaling? Anywhere from a few thousand dollars to tens of thousands of dollars, on up. My personal best for a wholesale fee on a contract is $50,000. It really depends on the deal itself, since you want to leave good money in the deal for the next investor. I'll show you some examples to illustrate my point.

A Good Wholesale Deal

A deal that's attractive to your buyer will have built-in money for them to make a nice profit. Your target audience will either be a rehabber, or a landlord, so your approach will vary only a little depending on which one. Here's a sample deal for a **rehabber**:

- Contract purchase price = $30,000. This is the amount you — or whoever you sell the contract to — will actually buy the house for.

- After Repair Value (ARV) = $65,000

- Rehab Costs = $11,000

- Wholesale/Assignment fee = $4,000 (Your profit)

- Total acquisition cost (before Closing costs) to the rehabber = $45,000

So here's the question you must ask yourself to determine if this process works. *Would I spend $45,000 total to acquire and rehab a $65,000 property?* If you would you'd make about $20,000 on this deal. You'd then have some holding costs, some taxes, and your selling costs. Let's say that they are 10% of the ARV total. That would leave you with $13,500 in profits ($20,000 minus $6,500 = $13,500).

Frankly, no rehabber would pass up this deal, because you've left it a good deal by not getting too greedy with your assignment fee. A $20,000 profit is a nice chunk of change. Think about this for what it really is… *You are selling money at a discount!* There should always be enough room in the deal for your buyer to make enough profit for the deal to be worth his while.

On your side it's a good deal, too. Very little capital or

work was required on your part, you didn't have to close on the property. You didn't have to do the rehab. And you made $4,000 for your efforts.

What does a deal that's unattractive to a potential buyer look like? Like this:

- Contract purchase price = $40,000

- After Repair Value (ARV) = $65,000

- Rehab Costs = $11,000

- Wholesale/Assignment fee = $10,000

- Total acquisition cost (before Closing costs) to the rehabber = $61,000

You see? There's only $4,000 left over for the rehabber, not including Closing costs, holding costs, advertising costs, or Realtor commissions to sell the property. He's probably actually in a negative position and will either sell the property at a loss, or have to try to sell it for more than it's worth. That's not exactly selling money at a discount, right? Remember, we need to leave money in the deal for the next investor; or else the deal won't work for him.

So what about landlords? How does this work for them? Well, it's pretty much the same. However, the math works a little more in your favor. The landlord is looking for a different outcome than the rehabber is. The rehabber cares about profits and the landlord cares about *cashflow*. Now, these two words may appear to be the same thing at first glance but they're not. Let's take a look at the actual definitions of these words:

- **Profit:** *A positive gain from an investment or business operation after subtracting for all expenses.*

- **Cashflow:** *Cash receipts minus cash payments over a given period of time.*

So, the rehabber is looking for a capital gain, or profit after he puts his money and time in, based on the sale price of the property. This is known as a cash-on-cash return, usually expressed as a percentage. The landlord is looking for a monthly return, based on the rents of a property, meaning if the rent is $700 per month, and the mortgage, taxes, insurance, reserve and property management equals $500, then the cashflow is positive, and equal to $200. Cashflow is expressed in real dollars.

If our goal is to cater to the landlord's needs, we'll need to position the deal a little differently. We do this simply by expressing the purchase and repair price as a monthly payment. In other words, if the property were 80% financed, the monthly payment would be the mortgage amount.

Let's look at how the first deal is positioned for a landlord. First we show the original numbers we gave the rehabber:

- Contract purchase price = $30,000.

- After Repair Value (ARV) = $65,000

- Rehab Costs = $11,000

- Wholesale/Assignment fee = $4,000 (Your profit)

- Total acquisition cost (before Closing costs) to the rehabber = $45,000

Then we position the property for the landlord:

- Mortgage at 80% LTV = $52,000

- Mortgage Payment (30 years at 7%) = $345.96

- Taxes = $112

- Insurance = $52

- Reserve = $35

- Monthly Rents = $700

- Monthly Cashflow = $155.04

- Instant Profit (Your cash-out refinance minus your acquisition cost of $45,000) = $7,000

So you see, in the rehabber's opinion this a good deal because the profit potential is about $20,000. From the landlord's perspective it's a good deal because he makes about $7,000 in profit plus $155 each month in cashflow for as long as he holds the property!

How does he make $7000 in profit, you ask? He simply borrows more money than he has put into the property. This is the same technique the late night infomercial gurus have been charging hundreds of dollars for their packages all these years. You remember… "And Johnny, I even got money back at Closing." The profit is actually a loan — tax-free — which the tenant will pay off. The landlord can also choose to borrow only the actual amount of money he has put into the property in return for a lower monthly payment. The difference in the mortgage amount is about $48 a month, but it would take about 12 years for that $48 to equal $7000.

So the only question left to answer is this: Would you buy a property if you didn't have to leave any of your own money in the deal, if it instantly gave you a $7,000 payday, and it provided you with residual income — cashflow — of $115 per month for life? Not to mention future wealth of $13,000 equity left in the property, or the reserve money you don't use — *plus* increases in the rental amount over the years! Would you really care if you paid me a $4,000 finder's fee for bringing you the deal? Of course not.

Getting Buyers

The last step to successfully wholesaling property is to have a bunch of willing buyers for your deals. We'll do this by building a "Buyers List." Start attracting potential buyers for your contracts by putting ads in the paper and going to local investor groups. These are places where people are looking for discount property.

Here's a successful newspaper ad I've been using for years:

HANDYMAN SPECIAL
3 BR/1.5 Bath Rental House
Roslyn Area, Good Schools
Must Sell NOW!
Call Joe at 215-555-4443

This ad drives people to call you looking for details on the property for sale. When they call, I give them property info, but I also ask investors what they are specifically looking to invest in. Rental and cashflow properties? Quick flip deals? Multifamily properties — duplexes, quads or small apartment buildings? I also find out what areas they want to buy in, as well as what price range they are looking in. Finally, I pre-qualify them from a financial perspective. I want to know what price ranges they buy in, and especially, how they will finance their purchase. If they are a cash buyer, they go straight to the top of my list. Hard money buyers are second, and traditional bank financing goes last.

It doesn't take a big budget here, just some willingness to do some short term work. Most of the people I sell wholesale deals to now are repeat buyers—and they are typically sold within 24 hours with no more than a simple e-mail to my Buyers List. My average wholesale fee is about $10,000 per contract. Selling just one wholesale deal a month can gross you over $120,000 per year!

You need all the same skills to wholesale a deal as you do to execute any other exit strategy. I highly recommend starting with this exit strategy if you are temporarily unable to do deals today for any reason. Wholesaling is a very lucrative way to learn, while you're doing things like building a cash reserve, fixing up your credit, or just working up the courage to do a deal for yourself. You'll learn by doing and get paid for the experience you're gaining along the way.

Exit Strategy 2: Retail the Property

This is also called "Fix and Flip," or selling a property on the retail market. You're going to buy the property, fix it up, and then sell it for a profit—above and beyond what you spent to buy it, hold it and rehab it.

To make this strategy work, you must buy the property right and do effective rehabbing. That doesn't just mean doing the fix-up work. It means running the numbers accurately and holding your General Contractor to a tight pricing and delivery schedule.

When you first go to look at the property, you'll want to compare it with comps to recently sold, similar properties in the area. Add 3-5% over the highest comp in an up market and decrease the number by 2% in a slow or down market. Once you commit to the project, meaning once you get your offer accepted, but before your due diligence period is over, it's time to get what's called an After Repair Appraisal. Why is this important? Well, certainty is the name of the game when doing retail projects. **We believe we make our money when we buy, not when we sell!** That means that we don't speculate or guess what the numbers will be. Consider this, if the property is not worth what you think it is, you'll immediately lose money as the property sits on the market for months waiting for a buyer or the marketplace to agree with you. That's not a position you want to be in.

I also require my Contractor to give me a detailed proposal on getting the property rehabbed — I call this a **Not-to-Exceed Quote.** Which means the price is the price, no matter what. It's up to my professional Contractor to know exactly what needs to go into the house, and to find any "surprises" before I settle on the property. Specifically, if wiring needs to be replaced, if there is mold, or hidden damage, I need to know about it and budget for it before I ever get to the Closing table. It is not acceptable for my Contractor to come back to me a few weeks into the rehab and say the job will cost more because of some hidden defect he didn't find until work started. This is called **Scope Creep** in the rehabbing industry, meaning the scope of the project continues to change until the only person making money on the deal is the Contractor.

The same holds true on the timeline for the project. If the Contractor quotes a completion date of eight weeks, I expect the job will take no more than eight weeks. I'll show you how I do this later in this chapter.

Getting the property sold

There are many ways to get your property sold. You can put out little signs at big intersections, and those road-signs that list your business name, website, and phone number. You know the signs I mean — developers use them all the time for new homes. You can also take out ads in those little free magazines that list properties for sale in your locale. You can consider listing the property in the newspaper. You may also decide you want to set up a website showcasing your properties, and you can give the URL in your newspaper advertisement.

However, none of these methods are for me. I call these the "do it yourself" (DIY) methods of selling property, and I'm way too lazy for that!

The truth is, the MLS is probably the best way to get your property noticed by the most people, but you'll have to go through a Realtor. This is by far, my preferred method of selling property. Why? Because there is no way you can live the Real Estate Lifestyle if you're busy conducting your own open houses every Saturday and Sunday while your family is sitting around wondering where you are. The Real Estate Lifestyle is about taking your time and your life back. If you take the DIY approach, you're letting the least qualified person — YOU! — do the job of highly trained professionals, so you're immediately guaranteed a steep learning curve, and a mediocre, if not sub-par result.

Really, you don't have to pay an arm and a leg to get a Realtor to sell your property, either. Many Realtors who are very good at marketing homes will list your property, actively market it, attend open houses, and even show the property at night during the week for less than 6%. My Realtor does this for me at 4.5% of the actual sale price. This is called an incentive or performance basis of being paid and that's how Realtors work. I never try to "cheap out" on my Realtor. I provide a continuing source of revenues on a performance only basis. When my Realtor sells a property for me, I immediately reward them with the next listing or property to sell. I do not shop around for a discount broker to sell my property cheaper. Instead, I build the Realtor's fees into my original numbers when I buy the property. I subtract his fees from my profit number and readjust my income expectations.

So, if I expected to sell a property for $190,000 and I have $140,000 in costs including purchase price, rehab, holding costs, and Closing costs, I'd expect to make $50,000 in profit. If I subtract my Realtor's charges at 4.5% of the sale price of $190,000, which equals $8,550, my new profit number becomes $41,450. The only question left to ask yourself is whether a $41,450 profit is acceptable to you if everyone else does all the work. A simple "yes" answer in my book.

I know you still must be thinking if you spend over $8,500 on a Realtor, that's a lot. However, you'll definitely be paying something even if you don't use a Realtor. Most people use a Realtor to purchase their homes, and their Realtor will need to be paid by someone. If you are not willing to pay the buyers' Realtor, odds are they will be buying someone else's property…not yours.

Now that we know you'll already be paying at least half of the $8,550 (or $4,275), what about the other half? Well, if you can't sell the property quickly you still have costs. First, you have the cost of the $140,000 sitting in the property, either not earning you interest, or you are paying interest on it. If it takes you an extra month or two to sell the property you're losing money. Worse yet, if the buyer negotiates a discount from you on the property it'll cost you even more! Realtors are skilled negotiators without the emotional baggage of being the guy with the money in the deal. The Realtor will be willing to play hardball, when you're ready to do anything to sell the property. In short, a professional Realtor will make you a lot of money because selling homes is his primary business. Use one!

Okay, we've explored the value of working with a Realtor to sell your property, so here's how to manage one. Be sure you gauge your Realtor's marketing success with a Weekly

Listing Activity Report. You need to know which methods are bringing you prospective buyers and which are not. If you're paying to run an ad, but you're not getting calls, drop that ad immediately! Of course, this means your Realtor needs to ask buyers how they heard about our property, so make sure that they do.

You want to know how many people responded to advertising, how many walked through the property, what objections did your Realtor hear (price, location, or features) and how many offers were submitted on the property from qualified buyers. You can't change the location of the property, but you can tweak the features and the price. I'd tweak the price last, assuming you have an appraisal in hand at or above your listing price.

What can you do if the property isn't selling?

If time goes by and your property just isn't moving, you need to figure out why and fix the situation. Start by analyzing your Realtor's marketing. If you don't know what their marketing is, call them up and ask. Find out anything and everything they're doing to get you a buyer for that property. If you're not satisfied, talk to them about making changes. Most Realtors will cooperate and do their best to satisfy you. But on the off-chance they won't cooperate, you might want to yank that listing and find another Realtor.

Another thing you must look at is your asking price. You may have been overly optimistic about what you thought you could get. In that case, you'll need to come down a bit.

Let's look at a few scenarios and see how the numbers go.

Example #1: Retail property sale

- After Repair Value — $175,000 (Based on Appraisal)

- Listing price — $169,500 (Priced for quick sale)

- Purchase amount — $94,000 (Including Closing costs)

- Rehab costs — $21,000 (Not-to-Exceed price)

- Gross profit potential = $54,500

However, you must factor in:

- Realtor's commission = $8,475 (5% of sale price)

- Closing costs = $5,085 (Estimated at 3%. Your Realtor will provide the exact amount.)

- Carrying costs = $1,675 (3 months @ $560, which includes taxes, insurance, etc.)

- Buyer negotiates sale price reduction (2%) = $3,390

In the deal above, you bought the place for $94,000 all in, and the comps were running about $175,000. At this point, you were probably salivating. But hold on. If rehab costs are $21,000 and we list the property for quick sale at $169,500, your profit potential is now:

$169,500 — $94,000 — $21,000 = $54,500

BUT, that's not all there is to it. You still have to pay the Realtor's commission of $8,475, the $5,085 Closing costs, and the costs of owning ("holding") the property while you rehab it — costs like taxes and insurance of $1,675. If the buyer makes an offer expecting 2% to help with his Closing costs (known as Seller Assist) it will cost you another $3,390. So the real profit potential is more like your potential profit minus those costs I just laid out for you:

$54,500 — $8,475 — $5,085 — $1,675 — $3,390 = $35,875

So you must decide for yourself whether the deal is worth it for a profit of $35,875. If you're just starting out, it probably is. The average salary for 80% of the American population is below $70,000 per year. In one deal you've just made six months' salary. On average this deal should take about three months from start to finish.

Example #2: Retail property sale using Hard Money

Let's take a look at the same example a different way. Suppose you don't have the money to get into this deal. Many people would walk away from this deal because it's "too big" for them. They don't have the $94,000, or the $21,000 rehab, so they **assume** that the deal is not for them. Let's look at the word assume:

ASS–U–ME

Enough said! You can take a few other approaches to this deal. But let's look at the most expensive option available to you—Hard Money. If you'll remember we talked about using Hard Money in the Financing section of this book. Let me show you how it works in an example using the same deal.

- Same gross profit potential: $54,500

- Same additional costs: $8,475 – $5,085 – $1,675 – $3,390

- Actual profit potential = $35,875

Now, let's subtract the costs of Hard Money. A Hard Money Lender will charge you 5 points up front and 15% interest for the loan. That may seem like a lot, but let's reserve our judgment for now. The 5 points and 15% is calculated on the actual loan amount, which may be up to 70% of the appraised value of the property. That amount may be over the actual costs needed to purchase the property and do all the work! That's 100% financing for your project, meaning no money — zero dollars — out of your own pocket!

You see, on an appraisal of $175,000, many Hard Money Lenders can loan you 75% LTV which equals $131,250. To do this deal in reality, you only need the $94,000 purchase price and Closing costs, plus the rehab price of $21,000. So on this deal the loan amount needed is only $115,000.

But we're not done yet. To pay the 5 points on the deal you need $5,750 and then three or four months of 15% interest, we can roll that money into the original loan. Let's use four months as a worst case scenario. That's an additional $1,437 per month or $5,748 in interest only payments for the four months. The total amount you'll actually borrow now is $126,498. That leaves an additional $4,752 you could have borrowed, but you don't need.

So how does Hard Money affect our profit scenario? Let's look:

- Actual profit potential = $35,875

- Hard Money Costs = $11,498 (That's 5 points at $5,750 + 15% Interest at $5,748)

- New profit potential = **$24,377**

So what do you think? Is this a good deal for you? You've used Hard Money, and no money of your own to do the deal and yet you've put $24,377 in your pocket in just four months. Just doing three of these deals a year is worth an additional $73,131 in your pocket in a single year! Would you still need to work?

The other good thing about Hard Money lenders is they

judge your credit-worthiness based on your deals, not your ability to repay the loan. That means once you have some experience doing deals like this, they will happily loan you money to do more than one deal at a time. If you could do just six of these deals in a year you could make almost $150,000. It's a lot easier than you think!

That's why retailing properties is one of my favorite exit strategies to use!

Exit Strategy 3: Renting with the Option to Buy

Renting out the property and giving the renter the option to buy it after a predetermined period of time, also known as Lease Optioning the property, is another way you could go. Simply; this is a lease-purchase. It is a combination of renting and selling the property. Two documents which I use cover this type of transaction. First, the Residential Lease, which governs the tenants staying at the property; how much rent will be paid, what happens if rent is late or unpaid, the condition the property will be kept in, and who's responsible for utilities. If the tenant defaults, a simple eviction is all that's required and my Property Manager can handle it. I don't use a fancy document for this function, just the state Association of Realtors standard lease.

The second document I use is a simple Option Agreement. First, let's define what an option is. An option is simply a document that gives a party the right to buy something or sell something before or on a certain date, at a certain price. As part of a lease option this simply means that for a certain fee, the tenant now has the right to buy your property at a particular price, so long as they keep the covenants of the Residential Lease—meaning, paying the rent on time—and they can acquire the financing to buy the property by a certain date in the future, usually one to two years.

This document is quite simple and can be drawn up by any Real Estate Attorney for just a few hundred dollars. Simply put, it should include the following:

1. How much the fee is for the option? We purposely call this fee a Nonrefundable Option Consideration, or NROC. This fee is NOT a deposit towards the purchase of the house, but simply the fee you are selling the option for. If the tenant breaks the Option Agreement, the Residential Lease, moves out, or you have to evict him, you get to keep the NROC.

2. By what date does the tenant need to prove he's acquired the financing to buy the property? If this date is missed, you can choose to charge an additional fee to extend the Option Agreement, or simply declare it null and void. I like to introduce the tenant to a mortgage broker right away so they can find out what they need to do to correct their credit situation over the course of the Option Agreement, so they can get a mortgage. This step almost guarantees they'll be able to close on the property in the specified time period.

3. On what date, come hell or high water, does the option expire? This date is critical. An open-ended option — no termination date — can be a nightmare because the tenant can then sue you if you try to sell the property and arbitrarily terminate the agreement.

It's important for me to underscore here that I don't subscribe to applying the tenant's rent payments towards buying the property. That's because I am voluntarily agreeing that for as long as that tenant has an Option to purchase my property, I can't sell it during the Option period — regardless of the market condition, or if I get an offer from another buyer for more money than the Option price is for. Any appreciation in the property belongs to the tenant when they exercise their option, so if the property goes up in value by 20% that is to the benefit of the tenant and not to me. There are plenty of benefits to me, though, so you won't hear me complaining.

One big advantage of lease optioning: you still get to take depreciation on the property while you hold the deed, which you do until the tenant has paid for the property.

However, occasionally, you'll run into a savvy tenant who's been warned about lease-purchase agreements, and they'll want to do a Contract for Deed. You, as the property owner/landlord, would prefer to do a lease-purchase since it offers you the option to evict them if they violate the agreement, and since you can still take depreciation. But a Contract for Deed (CFD) can work as a second choice.

A CFD is an agreement in which they agree to make payments over a period of time, and at the end of the period, if they have satisfied the provisions of the agreement, they get the deed. In the meanwhile, it's best to escrow the deed.

You will also want to record this CFD with the county, at the Recorder's office, immediately — then if there are improvements made to the property — which the tenants/buyers can do — and the Contractors aren't paid, they can file a materials lien against the property. So, if the tenants/buyers are shady and try to sell it out from under you before the term expires, the Contractors get paid first if you haven't recorded the CFD. If you have, then you come first.

One bad thing about a CFD is you can't take depreciation, but the tenants/buyers can. A good thing is you can usually require a much larger down-payment on a CFD than with a lease-purchase (LP). So run the numbers, and make up what you'll lose in depreciation with a higher down payment!

A great thing about both lease optioning and CFD is the tenant will take much better care of the property than if he's just plain renting it, because with a lease option or CFD, it's HIS property.

Example #1: Lease Optioning a Property

For this example, let's use a lower-end property worth $100,000 today. We've acquired the property for $62,000 including Closing and holding costs with a rehab price of $9,000. All in we now have $71,000 invested in the property. Now we'll go to the bank and refinance the property so we can move our money into the next deal. The bank gives us a loan on the property at 75% LTV, so we borrow $75,000 — that's an immediate $4,000 tax-free profit! — using the property as collateral.

We'll need to pay the loan back with on time payments over 30 years at 7.5% interest, so our monthly payment on the property is $525 each month. Next we have Real Estate taxes at $1,100 per year or $92 per month. Finally in the expense column we have our homeowner's insurance at $900 per year or $75 per month. The market rent for the area this home is in is $1,250 per month. We'll pay our Property Manager (more on that in the Rental section of this chapter) 10% of the gross rent to handle everything for us, so that's another $125 per month.

The deal now looks like this from an Asset and Liability standpoint:

- Property Value is $100,000

- Purchase and Rehab costs are $71,000

- Amount Borrowed is $75,000

- Cash-out refinance Profit is $4,000

- Equity (Future Profit) is $25,000

Now let's look at our Income and Expenses:

- Monthly Rental Income is $1,250

- Monthly Loan Payment is $525

- Monthly Taxes are $92

- Monthly Insurance is $75

- Monthly Property Management is $125

- Total Monthly Expenses are $817

- Total Monthly Profit (Cashflow) is $433 per month

By the way, this is the same basic math you need to know to hold the property and rent it out for cashflow. Now let's look at the Option part of our deal, using a one-year expiration on the Option.

- Non Refundable Option Agreement (NROC) is $10,000

- One-year positive cash flow is $5,196 ($433/mo x 12 months)

- Cash from sale is $25,000 ($100,000 – $75,000)

- Loan Amortization over one year is $691.38 (the amount of the loan that's been paid down)

- Gross profit potential is $10,000 + $5,196 + $25,000 + $691.38 = $40,887.38

Remember we also did a cash-out refinance by borrowing $75,000 instead of the $71,000 we had invested in the property, so we have an additional $4,000 in tax free profits from the loan. That brings our grand total gross profit on this Lease Option deal to **$44,887.38!** In my opinion this a great deal. We invested only time in this deal, but none of our own money. And we had very minimal exposure to any type of financial loss, such as not being paid the rent. We were paid on the refinance, we were paid on the option, we were paid cashflow, we were paid on amortization and we were paid on the sale!

My point explaining Lease Options to you first was not to sour you on renting out properties, not by a long shot. Renting out properties is the way I support my Real Estate lifestyle, secure my retirement income, and create velocity of money, like the Rich do. Let's discover what else you need to know to do the same.

Exit Strategy 4: Renting the Property For Cashflow

This is the game of the Rich in a nutshell. Renting properties for cashflow is an outstanding way to make money in Real Estate and has numerous advantages. You make money four different ways:

- Cashflow — The difference between what you get in rent and what you have to pay out in loan payments, taxes, insurance and repairs.)
- Depreciation you take on your taxes each year.
- Appreciation over time — The property is worth more 10 years down the line.
- Equity Increase or Amortization — What this means is your tenants are buying the property for you since you are using their rent money to make the mortgage payments.

Obviously, if you're renting the property for cashflow you'll need to get a tenant in there. *No tenant, no cashflow!* This is where the panic creeps in. Some people are cheap and think they should do their property management on their own. To me, this is plainly foolish. I am uniquely qualified to make that statement, because I was one of those people. To save a 7% to 10% management fee, I would actually screen my own tenants, try to fix their toilet problems, and I would personally go door to door trying to collect my rents. I could not have found a more frustrating and unproductive way to spend my time, if I tried.

I used For Rent signs, I used newspaper ads, I used online classifieds, I used flyers in churches and hospitals. I tried it all, but I still found myself scrambling to get tenants, and collecting from them was even worse. I was at a Real Estate Investor Association meeting complaining about this and asking people for suggestions. It turned out that many other people felt the exact same way. They were sick of being landlords, but had no idea how to correct the problem. That's when a far more experienced investor asked me the following question. "Why did you get into Real Estate? To be a landlord? Or to be an investor?" I explained I wanted to be neither. I just wanted to be Rich! That's when he asked me, "Which one of the two get Rich? Landlords or Investors? Rent Collectors or Donald Trump?"

This was my personal wake-up call. I wasn't making money in Real Estate and I was wasting my time and my life doing menial tasks that didn't make me money. I was losing way more than 10% by doing my own landlord work!

So if you're not going to do it, how do you find good tenants and keep the property in good repair? Enter the Property Manager!

Property Managers to the Rescue!

Property Managers are people who professionally handle your property for you. This is their only business and they are usually very good at it. Here's what I learned; I've been in the Real Estate investing business for nearly a decade now. My Property Manager, on the other hand, has been managing properties for more than 25 years. She has an assistant in the business for over 10 years. The office is run by someone in the business for over 40 years. That's 75 years of combined total experience. I'd have to live past 100 to trump that amount of experience! I wonder what made me think I could do a better job when I was just starting out? That's why I strongly recommend hiring a property management company.

What you want to look for is an independent company that specializes in managing commercial and residential properties. Why? Because when somebody specializes in something day in and day out, they're usually pretty darned good at it.

These people know their stuff. They've dealt with lots of tenants, they know what kinds of issues are likely to come up, and they know the best ways to deal with them. So let them handle it!

What responsibilities should property management take on for you? It depends on how much you want to pay. The Property Manager should be a licensed Real Estate agent. Some of them have a Broker's License, as well.

They begin by advertising the place for rent. The property management company should put out advertising and attract calls. They take the calls and show the place, and then they provide thorough screening of prospective tenants. When they find a good one, they will negotiate and execute the lease. They'll also take the security deposit and put it in an escrow account so the tenant knows it's safe and state laws are conformed to.

Prior to move-in, the Property Manager will do an itemized inspection. That means walking through the place, noting anything damaged and everything you are providing, such as a stove and any other appliances. The Property manager will also do the same thing at move-out.

The Property Manager will take all calls from tenants and arrange for repairs and maintenance. They will collect the rent and deal with delinquent tenants. If a tenant needs to be evicted, they'll handle that, too. They will also report evictions and unpaid rents or damages to credit agencies.

The property management company will also make timely rental income payments to you. Ask them what their timelines, scheduling, and processes are.

They will also be responsible for maintaining rents at market value. This means they will put in regular rent increases as leases expire or are renewed.

As far as the cost of repairs and maintenance, your Property Manager should get several competitive bids on any necessary work. You decide whether they should contact you before doing any work at all or if you want to set a dollar limit such as, "Anything under $250, just do it. Over $250, call for approval."

It's very important your Property Manager be accessible at least during business hours both for the tenant and for you. No voicemail hell. Ask them about that and then call them at different times to be sure. The Property Manager should also be able to handle listing and selling the property if you ask them. This is why it's nice to have a licensed Realtor manage the property. They will generally know lots of other investors and be able to speak to the rental history of the property.

You will want to have a contract with the property management company that spells out all these things and what/when they'll be paid, and most importantly, when you'll be paid. Most Property Managers have a management contract you'll find acceptable. The important thing is be sure payment is ALWAYS on a performance only basis, meaning if the Property Manager does not collect the rent, they DO NOT get paid. Period!

Even with a professional Property Manager in place, there are still some things you should know. We're into *delegating* responsibility, not abdicating it. So let's make sure we know what's supposed to happen and when.

Having **NO** tenant is better than having a **BAD** tenant

Bad tenants can cause you all kinds of problems. They can damage your property above and beyond what the security deposit covers — exceeding generally reasonable wear and tear. Check to see exactly what you can charge for a security deposit, since laws vary from area to area. Find out what the maximum is, and charge exactly that.

After advertising is placed in newspapers and elsewhere, then the prospective tenant calls the Property Manager, not you. If the tenant sounds OK over the phone, the Property Manager offers to show them the property. The Property Manager will then supply a Rental Application Form. What's important is to understand the process they'll use:

1. People call about the property.

2. Property Manager talks to them and pre-qualifies them over the phone.

3. Property Manager shows them the property.

4. If they like it, the Property Manager supplies an application form.

5. They fill out the form and give it back to the Property Manager, along with a fee to cover checking their credit.

6. The Property Manager checks and verifies the application thoroughly. That means calling all the telephone numbers to verify where they work, how long

191

they've been there, previous jobs, current landlord, prior landlord, and references.

7. If all that checks out, the Property Manager pays a service to check their credit, eviction report, and possibly their criminal history.

If things don't check out on the lease application, and it becomes clear the tenant has lied on the application, the Property Manager turns them down.

If everything does check out, then the Property Manager will call you, the owner, to discuss the qualified tenant. Ultimately the decision is yours as to who lives in your property.

Ask for any information you feel is relevant—credit score, income and ability to pay, pets, etc.

Now, I must be candid with you: if you're renting in a lower income neighborhood, you need to brace yourself when you get the credit report. Almost no one in a bad neighborhood has good credit, and most don't have OK credit.

That's why we use the Eviction Report and Income Verification as our primary standards in lower income neighborhoods. If you try to hold out for great credit, you just won't get any tenants.

So, if the applicant checks out and his credit is OK and you agree, then the Property Manager is ready to offer him a lease. My Property Manager likes to keep the first lease signed with a new tenant fairly short in case they don't work out. Twelve months is the absolute maximum.

Also, when they sign the lease, the Property Manager will collect the first month's rent, the last month's rent and the security deposit. My Property Manager requires these funds to clear before the new tenant gets keys, and moves in.

Again and again I hear stories about landlords who trusted a tenant to pay the security deposit over time, or after they moved in, and those landlords rarely if ever get that money. Make it simple: if they don't sign the lease, pay first month's rent, and pay the security deposit, they don't get the keys, period.

What's in a Lease, Anyway?

Now let's look at the contents of the lease. You can get a residential lease form now from a Realtor or Property Manager. Leases can be complicated and it's important you understand what they contain. Feel free to discuss your states' lease with your Property Manager.
Terms you'll find common to most leases:

1. **Parties/co-signers** — Anyone who signs or co-signs is on the hook for the rent and can be held liable for damages. If your tenant is a college student with no credit or job, you may want to insist his parents co-sign.

2. **Annual renewal term** — This clause says if nobody does anything, the lease renews itself after it expires. You have the option of modifying this clause to allow the rent to go up, and I recommend you do.

3. **Rents and additional rents** — This spells out exactly how much they'll pay each month, when it is due, and when it is late. It also tells them what the late fees are, and where and how to make payment on rent.

4. **Return of security deposits** — This is a required clause in most states. It says that when they move out you have 30 days to either return their security deposit or give them a written accounting of damages you had to use their deposit to cover. One thing you might want your

Property Manager to do is spend a little bit of time writing up a sheet of the usual and customary charges for certain damages that might occur, and give it to tenants when they move in. That way, they will not be so surprised when you deduct, say, $75 to replace a broken garbage disposal.

5. **Use and occupancy** — This clause says they will use the property for residential use only (not running a business.) It also lists everyone supposed to be living there.

6. **Landlord's right to enter** — Very important. It gives your Property Manager the right to enter the place with notice to inspect, repair or maintain.

7. **Appliances** — This sets forth exactly what appliances are to be included in the property for the tenant's use. I have heard of landlords recording the make and serial number, too, just to make sure the tenants don't move out of there with the good appliances you provided and leave crummy ones in their place.

8. **Utilities and services** — This usually itemizes who pays for what, such as electric, gas, water, garbage pickup, cable, etc. You should check either "Landlord" or "Tenant."

9. **Pets** — It's up to you whether or not you want to exclude pets, but whatever your policy is, you need to say. Bear in mind that most Americans own pets and if you do decide *not* to allow them, maybe because you just put in new carpet, well, you're losing more than half your market. My advice is to put in low-cost flooring and just collect an additional pet deposit of a few hundred bucks.

10. **Rules and regulations** — Tenant will abide by any

rules and regulations attached to the lease.

11. **Lead-based paint**—This discloses whether or not there is lead-based paint in the premises. Lead-based paint was phased out in 1978, so if the house was built after then it probably contains no lead paint. If it was built prior to 1978, it may or may not have lead paint. Lead paint is an issue because lead is poisonous and children have been known to eat paint chips.

12. **Destruction of property**—Tenant must let the Property Manager know if something's been destroyed or substantially damaged, or if there is a hazard that could cause severe damage. For instance, if a big tree limb is sagging

over the roof and looks like it's about to fall, tenant should let the Property Manager know.

13. **Insurance and release**—Tenants will buy their own insurance for their belongings and they will not hold you liable if something happens that destroys or damages their belongings.

14. **Breach/Notice to Quit**—Spells out what will break the lease agreement and how that will be handled. For instance, if the tenants start running a carry-out food business out of the house—which violates the Use and Occupancy section of the lease—they have breached the lease agreement and you can give them a Notice to Quit, which means they must move out within a certain number of days, usually 30.

15. **Tenant ending lease early**—Explains a process for the tenant getting out of the lease early, if you decide to allow that.

16. **Sale of property** — What happens if the property is sold during the lease period.

17. **Right to attorney** — Advises the tenant they have the right to an attorney and suggests they contact one if they have legal questions about the lease.

18. **Security deposits** — Goes into detail about how security deposits are taken, held, and under what conditions they are returned, and when.

Section 8 "Tenants"

People always ask me if I take Section 8 so I figured I'd include my opinion here. Notice the name of this section. A lot of people think that Section 8 is a special type of property. Not true. It's not about the property, it's about the tenants. Section 8 is a section of the Housing and Urban Development (HUD) code. It's designed to help out lower-income people who qualify for government assistance.

Why would you want to go through a bunch of government red tape to rent to lower-income people? Well, for one thing, Section 8 pays all or part of the rent, so there are no issues about getting the tenant to pay that part — the government pays it so you know you'll get it. Another good thing is the Section 8 portion of the rent is paid on time, every time.

And Section 8 may be a great choice if your property is kind of odd, like if it has two bedrooms or five since the most common numbers of bedrooms are one, two or four. You can sometimes get more rent for these types of properties with Section 8 than you normally would.

Of course, as with anything in this life, there are some drawbacks. Currently, Section 8 has a financial freeze on. This means rents for Section 8 landlords will not go up, and in some cases they may actually go down.

196

Very bad.

For another thing, Section 8 quits paying as soon as you file for eviction. And then it could take a few extra months to rent your unit because of all the bureaucratic things the Section 8 program must do to get a tenant in there.

To me, the worst thing is the government now runs your business and can tell you what to do.

Here's the process for getting started with Section 8 housing. You market the property in the newspaper and in the Section 8 list. However, to do Section 8, you must meet their requirements. You select a tenant just like you would any other tenant and fill out the landlord portion of the Section 8 voucher package. Then the real fun begins.

Section 8 will set you up with an inspector who will check your property to make sure it meets Section 8's standards. Here's the thing: you WILL fail that inspection the first time! Everyone does. It's a negotiation process with Section 8. You'll need to negotiate the rent with them. If they call you, it's a good sign you might be able to work something out.

When it comes time to sign the lease, Section 8 will call you and let you know they have what they need. Then you'll go to them to sign the lease.

Two real-world scenarios

I can talk about rentals all day long, or I can show you how it's done instead. In my opinion, it's very easy to understand how cashflow Real Estate works by looking at example properties and how the deals were structured. What I'll do next is provide two actual examples for you to follow along with so you can see how I determine my profit structures. Don't worry. I'm not going to show you a 60 unit apartment building in Manhattan that's out of your reach. Instead I'm going

197

to show you a few nice, easy deals representative of the kind anyone — even you — can do right now.

Cashflow Property #1

First, let me show you a duplex, which means the property has two apartments under one roof. This property is located on 630 South 51st Street in Philadelphia, Pennsylvania. The

configuration of the property is what's known as a 1 + 2, which means on the first floor, there is a one bedroom apartment. On the second floor is a two bedroom apartment. This property is located just outside a section of Philly called University City, an area that is dense with college students. The first-floor tenant goes to Temple University, and the second floor tenant is a math major at Drexel University. The upstairs tenant pays $700 per month, and the downstairs tenant pays $650 per month. The gross combined income on this property is $1,350 per month.

But before I get too far ahead of myself, let me tell you how I got this sweet deal.

I found out about this property from my Realtor on a Sunday afternoon. We had the property under contract by Monday afternoon, with no more than a $1 deposit and our written offer of $21,534.28, exactly what the owner owed the mortgage company that was getting ready to foreclose. This amount was the payoff amount for the mortgage which was four months in arrears. In my offer I also agreed to pay off the seller's back water bill of $1,609.48. People with these types of problems are what I call *motivated sellers*. Motivated sellers are always happy to give you a good deal on a property. You'll understand what I mean when you see the appraised value of the property.

So, I ordered an After Repair Value appraisal the very next day, and also sent my General Contractor in to estimate the repairs. **The Appraiser gave me a written value of $112,500!** The General Contractor's Not-to-Exceed quote came in at $42,053.20.

I bought the property and paid my Closing costs and rehab expenses with a few checks from my home equity line of credit (HELOC) just like I taught you in the section on financing.

Now, let's break down the deal again, looking at our Assets and Liabilities, and our Income and Expenses. First, on the acquisition side, getting into the deal, my cost breakdown was as follows:

Purchase Price	**$21,534.28**
Past Due Water Bill	$1,609.48
Closing Costs	$940
Transfer Tax (2% of Purchase)	$861.37
Rehab Price	$42,053.20
Total Acquisition and Rehab	**$66,998.33**

I closed on the property in the middle of February. The work on this project was completed in just about 45 days at the end of April. The Contractor did amazing work on this property. He separated all the electric and gas so I wouldn't have any ongoing expenses with the property besides the water bill and general maintenance. He put in new kitchens, bathrooms, carpets and windows. The dump of a house that I bought was a palace when I saw it the second time, just after the Contractor's repair work was completed.

I refinanced the house on May 2nd at 70% LTV on $112,500. My loan amount was for $78,750 even though my total costs to purchase and fix up the property were only $66,998.33. My interest rate for this loan is 7.25% using a 25 year amortization schedule. An amortization schedule is the breakdown over the life of the loan showing principal and interest repayments. The longer the amortization in years, the lower your monthly payment.

Appraised Value	**$112,500**
Loan Amount at 70% LTV	$78,750
Closing Costs on Loan	$1,951.62
My Actual Expenses	**$66,998.33**
Cash in My Pocket	$9,800.05
Free Equity To Me	**$33,750**

Let me give you a few more comments on the deal so far.

The *Cash in My Pocket* line is actual tax free profit to me because I was able to borrow more money on the property than I actually put into it. This is called a Cash-Out Refi. This is what I mean when I say "You make your money when you buy and not when you sell." The line called Free Equity to Me is the remaining equity in the property.

As you can see, I'm in a very safe position if I ever need to sell the property fast, because I could sell the property for $33,000 below its actual market value. Or I could sell it at its real market value and profit the same $33,000.

Of course I'd only sell this property if I absolutely had to! It's a money maker.

Now let's dig into the fun part: Making cashflow on the property. This is the money that finances my Real Estate Lifestyle. You'll quickly see it only takes a few of these deals to really upgrade your current standard of living and get back your free time by either working less, or recreating more.

My Property Manager handles the property for 7% of the monthly collections. The gross rent on the property is $1,350 per month. All the utilities except water are in the tenants' names as their responsibility to pay. On average, the water bill runs about $50 per month.

Annual property and school taxes on this property are a meager $846.33. That's why I love buying big-city properties. The reason Real Estate taxes tend to be so low in major metropolitan areas, excepting maybe Manhattan and San Francisco, is because of the sheer density of houses, meaning there are just so many houses, so cities can afford to make the taxes cheaper to attract more residents.

Finally, the insurance quote for the property came back at $713.50 per year.

Now, let's look at our Income and Expenses for this property on a monthly basis:

Gross Rents	**$1,350**
Property Management	$94.50
Monthly Mortgage Amount	$569.21
Monthly Property Taxes	$70.52
Monthly Insurance	$59.41
Monthly Water Bill	$50
Reserves	$50
Monthly Positive Cashflow	**$456.36**

Does this look like a good deal to you? It took about five hours of my personal involvement to do this deal. I got a FREE duplex. In fact, I got a tax free check for $9,800.05, because I was smart enough to do the deal. I also got $33,750 in FREE equity…AND if that weren't enough, I get $5,476.32 per year—an extra $456.36 every single month for the rest of my life, or until I get tired of getting checks just for owning the building!

That's not to mention increases in the value of the Real Estate — Appreciation at no less than 4% a year in my area until I sell it! -, and increases in the rents for both units which average about 5% each year in my area. In 25 years, when the mortgage is paid off my monthly cashflow increases to the full rent amount, less taxes and insurance. That's not to mention all the money that I put aside in reserves — $50 per month — I didn't have to use.

Now think about this for a minute. *The total profit on this deal in just one year is $49,026.37.* That's $9,800.05 cash-out re-finance + $33,750 in equity + $5,476.32 in cashflow from rents. All that money was created by using the knowledge I'm giv-ing you in this book and only five hours of my personal time invested.

If you're one of those skeptic types — like I was — and you think this is simply too much trouble to go through to make $456 each month, I want you to please consider something: How much is your car payment? I can buy a 2007 BMW 328i for about $450 per month! What would your life be like if you never had to make a car payment again?

How many of these deals would you need to never have to make another mortgage payment on your house? What if you never had to pay for your own groceries again? Or cable bill, or electric bill? This is what I mean by The Real Estate Lifestyle! I let the Real Estate pay for the stuff I want. I can do it, and you can do it, too.

Starting to get the hang of this now? Great! Because it's time for us to look at another cashflow property.

Cashflow Property #2

This time we'll look at a little single family home in a work-ing class neighborhood, located at 4802 Duffield Street in Philadelphia. The reason I'm showing you this deal is because it is so small and simple, anyone can do it. My personal time invested in the property was less than 4 hours, but the profits and ongoing cashflow are very exciting. This type of deal takes so little effort that, with the right team in place, it can be done in less than 60 days. It is not far-fetched to say you could easily do six of these deals a year and be well on your way to living the Real Estate Lifestyle in a very short period of time.

There are only a few moving parts to this type of deal, so it's very easy to create a cookie-cutter process to get them done quickly. What I mean by this is that you could do this same deal over and over again, with ease, and the only thing that would change is the address of the property.

So this 1,222-square foot rental house is a 3 bedroom, 1 bath row home in Northeast Philadelphia. In this area there are 40 identical houses on each and every block. They all have the same exact layout. When you walk in the front door, you are in the living room, then the dining room, then the kitchen. Upstairs are three bedrooms; a master bedroom that's larger and two smaller bedrooms. Finally, there is a full bathroom, complete with sink, toilet and shower.

This is a very vanilla deal, without a sexy story. The deal came about just from putting previous offers on houses in the neighborhood. This home was on the market for just over 200 days when I made my offer. The seller was a bus driver and his wife, a city police officer. They were separated and in the process of getting divorced, so the house was a marital asset that needed to be sold. Again, a highly motivated seller.

The property was in great condition, except it needed a clean-out, new paint, new carpets and a new roof. It already had a brand new heater, a new hot water heater, new electric and plumbing. The total rehab costs were $6,000.

Since I did most of the explaining with the first example, I'll give you the essentials to this deal right up front. First the costs to acquire the property:

Purchase Price	**$30,000**
Closing Costs	$1,010.49
Transfer Tax (2% of Purchase)	$600
Rehab Price	$6,000
Total Acquisition and Rehab	**$37, 610.49**

After the rehab was complete I applied to refinance the property. The property was appraised at $55,000. Here's what the Assets and Liabilities look like for this deal:

Appraised Value	**$55,000**
Loan Amount at 80% LTV	$44,000
Closing Costs on Loan	-$800
My Actual Expenses	**-$37,610.49**
Cash In My Pocket	*$5,589.51*
Free Equity to Me	**$11,000**

Now let's look at our Income and Expenses for this property on a monthly basis. The rent for this property is $750 per month. The property management costs me 7%. The loan is at 80% LTV with a 6% interest rate on a 30-year amortization. Annual Real Estate taxes are $473.36 and annual insurance is $511.08.

Gross Rents	**$750**
Property Management	$52.50
Monthly Mortgage Amount	$263.80
Monthly Property Taxes	$39.44
Monthly Insurance	$42.59
Reserves	$25
Total Expenses	$423.33
Monthly Positive Cashflow	**$326.67**

Here's my profit scenario for this property. Because I bought the property right and was able to do a cash-out refinance, I immediately put **$5,589.51** in my pocket tax free. And with income at $750 per month and expenses at $423.33 I pocket another $326.67 each month, or **$3,920.04** each year. I also got another $11,000 in equity. My grand total profit on this little row home was **$20,509.55.**

All of that money comes from a little bit of general knowledge, a plain-vanilla deal with no special bells and whistles and only a few hours of my personal time and involvement. If you follow the path I've laid out for you in this book, the Real Estate Lifestyle will soon be yours.

Now let's talk about the icing on the cake. The stuff that makes my richest students so successful. It's really the "secret ingredient" that makes the difference between the real winners and those who wish they were winners.

Chapter 12: What's Your Real Estate Lifestyle?

The Rocket Fuel That Makes All of This Work

What's Your Real Estate Lifestyle?—
The Rocket Fuel That Makes All of This Work

You've probably heard you won't succeed if you don't set goals and write them down. But most people don't write down their goals because either they won't find the time, or because they simply don't know what their goals are.

This is a which-comes-first, chicken-or-egg situation: if you don't know what your goals are, how can you write them down? So you don't even bother to try.

Or maybe you've sat down on a few occasions and written out some goals like:

- Make more money
- Be financially secure
- Own my own business

These goals are a good start, but unfortunately they just aren't specific enough. How much money is more, exactly? A hundred more dollars every month? Five hundred? A thousand? The problem with a vague goal is that it has too much wiggle room. You don't know when you've achieved the goal, if you can't measure and quantify it. In the case of more money, you could get really lazy and claim victory on an extra ten bucks a month. Or you could make tons of money and still be miserable, because you've never defined how much is enough.

The main excuse I hear for not writing down goals is people don't have time. Let me ask you something: if there was something you could do that would only take five or 10 minutes a day and was guaranteed to increase your odds of success 100-fold, would you do it?

Years ago, a business coach of mine taught me there are 86,400 seconds in each day—no more, no less. In that amount of time, some people become President of the United States. Others become Rich and powerful. Some become Bill Gates, or Donald Trump or even Mother Theresa. Others do nothing. They work their tails off making someone else Rich. Or they spend their time wishing they were someone else. Others still spend that time blaming other people for their situations. What will you do with your 86,400 seconds?

Here's what I know: Write down your goals, and then your actions will start to line up with those goals. You'll be amazed to discover how much free time you suddenly have. *Setting goals helps you become more efficient.*

But those goals must be specific. Most people just write they want "more" of this and "more" of that. The same business coach of mine also taught me **a goal is just a dream with a date on it.**

Instead of "make more money," write down how much more money you want to make, by when, doing what. Instead of "achieve financial freedom," get specific and write down "Generate $6,000 a month in passive income with residential Real Estate by January 1, 2009." When you do that, you know exactly what target you're shooting at and how far away you are. You can measure the goal.

Another thing you want to do is to **categorize** your goals. Most people confuse business goals with financial goals—they're not the same. What's the difference, you ask? Well, a business serves its owner, not the other way around. Businesses don't exist so the employees can have a job, or so that customers can have a convenience. Businesses exist to serve the owner.

Your business represents what your money is doing for you. And in that business, there's your job, and then there is your money's job. In the Real Estate investing business, **your**

job is to discover and set up profitable deals. Your **money's job** is to provide the capital for those deals.

Do you see the difference? If you put things in their proper categories, they are much easier to compartmentalize, manage, and therefore, **galvanize**!

What sort of categories am I talking about?

- Personal goals, including leisure
- Family goals
- Social goals
- Legacy/spiritual goals
- Health goals
- Business goals
- Financial goals

Combine these seven areas, and you get your personal Real Estate Lifestyle. Why? Because you can use Real Estate as the vehicle to attain the money and free time that you need to accomplish any goal in any category. Keep that in mind as I explain each category for you.

Personal goals include financial freedom, living in a certain kind of house, having a pool, a certain car, etc. Your personal goals will drive your business and financial goals. For me, it's all about lifestyle. Sure, I love money, sure, but more importantly, I love what it does for me. If I spend all my time making money, I'd be sick from the constant high stress. I need my leisure down-time and recreational activities.

Family goals are important, too. Do you want to spend more time with them? Family goals are the opposite of leisure goals—they're very selfless. When you ignore family goals, you create stress and pressure at home. And if you have that, there's no way you'll be able to succeed. So what are your goals for your family? Things to do together, places to see, experiences to have together. The shared stuff that makes memories!

Social goals are another category. They have to do with your social standing and how you are seen in the community. Do you want to be President of the Homeowner's Association or Country Club? Do you want to get into public speaking, maybe? These goals have to do with your circle of friends, associates, and your level of influence.

Health goals are tough for business owners. We frequently neglect them, with bad results. For me, I want to live to be 100, but there's a problem — I smoke cigars. That's inconsistent, I know, so I'm going to have to address it if I want to be a Real Estate geezer!

Then there are your **Legacy** and your **Spiritual** goals. One particular American Indian tribe based their decisions upon how it would affect the people seven generations down from them. These Native Americans were concerned with their legacy, and you can bet they made some pretty thoughtful decisions because of that! As for your **spiritual** goals, you'll need to decide on those for yourself.

As we discussed earlier, we also have **Business** and **Financial** goals.

I'll help you get started. On the next page is a goal sheet. Make copies of it and fill it in. Since I couldn't give you homework in the Exit Strategies section because you need to have a deal in hand, consider this the homework you hoped I forgot about.

Make sure you put dates on your goals. Most people write their goals in terms of one to three years. You rarely see people writing down five, 10, 15 or 20-year goals. It's the vision thing — you have to have a vision for your future. Destination? Or Destiny? If you don't know where you're going, you're liable to end up just any old place. Why not put yourself in control of where you end up?

Homework: What's Your Ultimate Real Estate Lifestyle?

Be as specific as possible!

Today's date _____

   1. Personal Goals: _____
   _____

   2. Family Goals: _____
   _____

   3. Social Goals: _____
   _____

   4. Legacy/Spiritual Goals: _____
   _____

   5. Health Goals: _____
   _____

   6. Business Goals: _____
   _____

   7. Financial Goals: _____
   _____

Translating your Goals into Reality

Once you've got your goals written down, you've got to get there. Lots of people say they want something...like to make a million dollars, but when the rubber hits the road, they don't take action towards achieving that goal.

They don't take the necessary steps.

Suppose I held a $100 bill in front of you and asked if you wanted it. "Sure," you'd say. But are you really willing to do what it takes to get it?

Time for you to become a person of action. Half-measures just won't cut it. You need to commit yourself to taking action. Don't let fear derail you. Fear of what? Failure? Embarrassment?

Get over it.

When you work at a job for someone else, you commit to coming in each day at a certain time and doing certain agreed-upon tasks in exchange for a paycheck. So why should it be any different when you work for yourself as a Real Estate investor?

What you need, besides initiative, is accountability. When you're in business for yourself, you are only accountable to yourself. If you write down your goals and lay them aside, never to look at them again, you're the only one who knows.

You're cheating yourself!

I know it's scary to go out into the world and step forward on your own, but you've got to do it. Trust me, Real Estate investing provides one heck of a nice lifestyle, but you've got to get there first. You've simply got to get off your butt and take the necessary steps.

It really is that simple.

Managing Fear

There's no difference between wealthy people and you — they just got over their fear. You must get over fear, too.

What does fear look like? It looks like…

- "If I buy this property, it will fall down and I'll be stuck with a dog."
- "If I try to sell this house no one will ever buy/rent it."
- "I'll fail and be a loser."
- "People will laugh at me."
- "I've never had much money, so why will things be any different?"
- "I'm a loser."

Get over it! Let me make it really simple. Rich people think all the same things. We simply act in spite of our fear! The voices in your head are not real — they are fabricated by your subconscious mind. Tell the voices of fear to just shut up already. You've got work to do!

Anyone who really has a hard time dealing with the chatter in your head, I highly recommend Rich Dad Advisor Blair Singer's "Little Voice Management System." You can get a copy on his website (www.salesdogs.com).

Let me share with you one of my favorite quotes concerning fear:

"So, first of all, let me assert my firm belief that the only thing we have to fear is fear itself — *nameless, unreasoning, unjustified terror* which paralyzes needed efforts to convert retreat into advance."

Franklin Delano Roosevelt
His First Inaugural Speech
Saturday, March 4, 1933

Your Plan

You can become a successful Real Estate investor in as little as an hour each day. All you need is the proper Action Plan and the willingness to follow it. You have a seven-day week, six days for your Action Plan and one day you take off, and don't do anything Real Estate-related. For me it's Sunday. Refresh yourself; connect with family and friends; recharge.

MONDAYS: When you come home from work, take time to greet your family and eat dinner. After that, get on the computer and look at listings for an hour. Don't do this at your day job when you're supposed to be working — it's not ethical. Make Monday your "looking at listings" day. It's fine to do this just one day a week, because Real Estate doesn't move fast like the Stock Market. Be prepared to look at 80 or 100 listings in that one hour. Work expands to take up the time allotted to it. Set a timer and limit yourself to just one hour. If it takes you longer than that in a particular sitting, resolve to go faster next time and stop at one hour anyway.

TUESDAYS: On the way home from work, spend an hour doing drive-bys on the listings that you selected Monday. Saturdays, you'll look at properties. Set them up with Map Quest, use a GPS system, map them out efficiently. Make sure you don't waste time — if you're in that neighborhood by 6 PM, and then be out by 7 PM. Again, be strict about your time.

WEDNESDAYS: Spend a half-hour putting together an e-mail that says, "Dear Realtor, at 1 PM on Saturday I want to see the following properties." Always ask to see twice as many properties as you actually do want to see, and list the properties in order of priority. Then follow up with a phone call to your Realtor to confirm and make sure those properties have keys and lock boxes.

THURSDAYS: You can either prepare some offers for properties so if you decide to make an on-the-spot offer Saturday, you can do it. If you have no offers to make in your queue, spend an hour reading some personal development books from the Recommended Reading section of this book. Later on, when you have other activities like checking in on Contractors, you'll do those activities in this time slot.

FRIDAYS: If you haven't heard from your Realtor, call to double-check if everything is set up for Saturday. Set a deadline for a response and call again if your Realtor hasn't gotten back to you by the deadline. Make sure your Realtor and team members honor the commitments they make with you.

SATURDAYS: You'll spend a half-day walking through properties. Allow an hour for travel time, and you can probably expect to see about 15 properties. If you see something you like, make an offer on the spot. Remember: **Activity Drives Results!** Meet your Realtor at the first property and go from there.

Need motivation? You can't get results unless you start taing action! Don't go nuts at first—people tend to over-prepare for things. Don't over-complicate this very simple process.

SUMMARY: Your Real Estate Lifestyle Schedule

Monday—Spend an hour going through listings and selecting properties.

Tuesday—Spend an hour doing drive-bys on the properties you've selected.

Wednesday—Compose an e-mail to your Realtor itemizing all the properties you want to look at and more. List them in priority order.

Thursday—Either read or prepare offer letters for Saturday.

Friday—Double-check with the Realtor to make sure you're on for Saturday to look at all those properties.

Saturday—Spend a half day—three or four hours—looking at about 15 properties. Estimate your MAO for each. For the ones that look good, make an offer.

Sunday—Do not work on anything Real Estate related. Take off, rest, have fun, and connect with family and friends. Sharpen the saw by reading or otherwise educating yourself.

Chapter 13: Getting Started

Now It's Time to Do Something!

N ow that I've shared with you what I do, it's your turn. You really need to take your Seven Steps to financial freedom, one at a time. Nothing will happen if you don't take action.

So, in a gesture of unabashed generosity, I'm providing you with the ultimate Real Estate Lifestyle check-list, to get you started in earnest.

Someday you'll thank me.

Let me reassure you—you want this. You need this. And you definitely can do this. This isn't rocket science. It isn't even all that complicated. You don't need a college degree or a genius IQ to be a successful Real Estate investor—not even close.

All you have to <u>do</u> is follow my system, the simple step-by-step system I've laid out for you in this book. Now go back and read the fifth word of the last sentence: "do."

I can't guarantee what will happen if you take action, but I CAN guarantee what will happen if you don't: **NOTHING.**

Right here, right now, promise yourself out loud you **WILL** commit to taking the steps necessary to build a successful career in Real Estate. Pick a reasonable starting date, and commit to it.

Then—TAKE ACTION!

If you can start taking steps the very next Monday, great! If you're in the middle of something you have to see through—like moving, or a new baby coming soon—you may have to pick a later date.

That's OK. I'll forgive you, as long as you pick one.

Your Real Estate Lifestyle Action Check-List:

☐ Set up your business entity — This will probably be either an S Corporation or a Limited Liability Company (LLC.)

☐ Set up your financing — Find cash for buying properties, through some combination of personal savings, a home equity loan, private investment, bank loan, or hard money loan.

☐ Get a good Realtor and possibly a back-up Realtor — Even the best Realtors can get in a slump where they start letting you down, so it's a good idea to have a back-up. Treat your Realtor well, trust him, and he should do right by you.

☐ Set up some basic business forms, including offers and sales contracts — a Realtor should provide the basic ones, you can customize them. Once you've got your forms set up electronically, all you have to do is fill them in for each new property.

☐ Select a "farm" area — Make sure you narrow it down. An entire zip code is not a good farm area; it's too big. Keep it to a neighborhood. The idea is to have a small enough area so you can learn it inside out.

☐ Get set up to receive leads for listings — The Realtor can help you with this. You'll need to make sure you get leads and have listings ready to review each Monday.

☐ Set aside time to review listings every Monday — You need to make the commitment to spending the time necessary to do this. Tell yourself it's only an hour and just do it.

☐ Select properties to walk through — This is not hard to do, and after awhile you'll get a feel which roperties would be the best deals at what price.

☐ Make offers- this is the biggest stumbling block for new investors. Don't let fear hold you back. Conquer it! Make those offers. Overcome that inertia! ou won't get properties unless you do. It's as simple as that.

☐ Buy properties - If your offer is accepted and you're not currently over-committed, buy the property. Your Realtor and title company will line up a Closing for you.

☐ Set up a spreadsheet to keep track of peroperties and timelines - This won't seem critical at first, but believe me, once you start accumulating properties it's a must.

☐ Make money, prosper, live, love, and start living your own Real Estate Lifestyle!

Chapter 14: Final Thoughts

*Further Study—Developing
Your Business Brain*

Final Thoughts: Further Study—
Developing Your Business Brain

Recommended Reading

A s a Real Estate investor, your learning and growing never ends. Over the years I've found that reading books, attending seminars and availing myself of additional educational resources; such as Real Estate investing newsletters, audio and video materials, Coaching programs and networking groups have literally propelled me to amazing levels of competency in both my business and personal worlds.

You'll notice there are not any "how-to" Real Estate books on this list. That's because I'm holding that back for just a few more pages. Instead, this Recommended Reading list is loaded with books that will shift your paradigms and the way you think. All these books are in what I call my *Active Reading Library*. I've read all of them numerous times and they stay in the "rotation" of whatever I happen to be reading or studying at the time.

Remember, reading and learning are necessary, but not nearly as necessary as actually DOING the things that will help you to achieve your goals. *Living the Real Estate Lifestyle means living a program of action!* With that said, let's get on with the list and what you can expect to get out of each book.

Rich Dad, Poor Dad
What The Rich Teach Their Kids About Money—
That The Poor And Middle Class Do Not!
By Robert T. Kiyosaki with Sharon Lechter, CPA.

This book started it all for me, and millions of others. I remember the absolute exhilaration I felt when I learned there was a better way to get what I wanted out of life by learning how to make my money work for me instead of me working for money. If you haven't read it yet, make this book the <u>very next</u> book you read. It will put a lot of the concepts in my book into context for you and vastly improve your financial literacy.

Rich Dad's Prophecy
Why the Biggest Stock Market Crash in History Is Still Coming...
and How You Can Prepare Yourself and Profit from It!
By Robert T. Kiyosaki with Sharon Lechter, CPA.

Frankly, I recommend the entire "Rich Dad" series of books, but this book, Prophecy, is by far Robert's most important work. Written in 2001, Robert has predicted many things we're seeing in the macroeconomic and financial world today.... The Social Security crisis (with an anticipated 25 trillion dollar shortfall) and the Medicare mess (over 65 trillion dollars short), the impact of 78 million baby boomers retiring, rampant inflation, the arrogance and denial of the Federal Reserve Bank, and the devaluation of the American dollar against other world currencies.

These issues impact <u>all</u> Americans and will greatly shape future economic policy, therefore all investors – including your 401k. Rich Dad's Prophecy will help you to understand the financial world around you. Most importantly it will teach you how to prepare and profit when things happen in the financial markets. This is not a doom and gloom book. It is a gloom and boom book!

No B.S. Wealth Attraction for Entrepreneurs
The Ultimate, No Holds Barred, Kick Butt, Take
No Prisoners Guide to Really Getting Rich
By Dan S. Kennedy

What's amazing about this book is it came out months before "The Secret" and is, in my opinion, far more usable. I believe in Dan's work so much I'll be appearing in an Infomercial with him, and a whole host of others, promoting his new masterwork DVD called "The Phenomenon." Success leaves clues, and Dan Kennedy has been an outstanding model for me, as he's all about practical application.

This book doesn't just tell you that a "secret" exists; it tells you what the secret is, and then shows you how to use it and apply it to become wealthy. This book is destined to become the "Think and Grow Rich" of our time.

Secrets of the Millionaire Mind
Mastering the Inner Game of Wealth
By T. Harv Eker

Probably the most potent book in the world for understanding people's attitudes about money – even yours – and how to overcome them. I've been a student of T. Harv Eker's work since 2001, when his book called Speedwealth – How to Make a Million in Your Own Business in 3 Years or Less, a practical guide to launching and selling a business, was released. Following Harv Eker's business building principles, I sold my own Technology Consulting company in 2006 for a seven-figure return and got to keep 15% of the business and profits. His Millionaire Mind book will help you to see and understand your own "money make-up" as well as encouraging you to overcome old programming and limitations that may be holding you back. I recommend all of Harv Eker's work to anybody that will listen to me.

Trump: The Art of the Deal
By Donald J. Trump and Tony Schwartz

This book is the next step in a Professional Real Estate Investor's evolution. It's Donald Trump's personal account of how he came up through the ranks with his father and personal mentor Fred Trump. Starting with the low-income apartment complexes he managed in Ohio, through some of the most historic deals he did in New York City, he delves deeply into what he was thinking when he did each deal. There are many very instructive lessons in that book on creative negotiating, lateral thinking, and personal branding. As an aside, Trump's third book, "Trump: the Art of the Comeback," chronicles how he dealt with business bankruptcy and the disaster of the 1986 Savings and Loan bust. Another very instructive read, but not for the easily offended or the faint of heart.

Entrepreneurial Genius
The Power of Passion
By Gene N. Landrum, Ph.D.

As you can see by the rest of this recommended reading list, I'm not generally into dissertations by scholars. I prefer the "no guts, no glory" view of the world from people that actually build businesses and Real Estate empires. I prefer to read books by those that have "been there and done that" in application, not theory. That's why I was surprised when a millionaire friend of mine turned me onto a book by a Ph.D. It turns out that Gene Landrum is actually one of us...The guy invented and launched the Chuck E. Cheese chain of children's entertainment restaurants despite terrible opposition – Hey, who's going to come to a restaurant with a rat as a spokesman? – And yet he achieved heralded acclaim and billions in revenues!

That's why his book is so important. He looks at the success stories of a dozen hardcore entrepreneurs and identifies exactly what made them successful through his own "special case," as Buckminster Fuller would say. People like Henry Ford, Coco Chanel, Michael Dell, Hugh Hefner and Richard Branson are profiled — not just their achievements, but the psychology, attitudes and belief systems that make them different from most people. It's absolutely amazing how much these people all have in common with each other and how similarly they viewed the conventional thought and societal norms most people follow. I really hope Gene Landrum does Part Two of this book one day.

World renowned Success Speaker and Business Coach Jim Rohn is credited with having said "Rich people have big libraries. Poor people have big TVs. It's not coincidental." A final word of advice: Invest in your personal education and development, every single day of your life! But don't let all that knowledge sit on your bookshelf. Apply that information immediately by taking Massive Action. An expanded Recommended Reading List as well as what I'm reading now, who I'm learning from, and how I'm using that information in my businesses and Real Estate can be found on my website at **www.livetherealestatelifestyle.com.**

Discovery Versus Invention

Let's talk quickly about the subject of discovery versus invention. I see, buy, and study lots of Real Estate investor books and courses every year. Strangely, it's a rare occasion when the author of one of these courses gives credit to the people that taught them the strategies they're teaching. It's a fact that we all discover "new" ways to do things from other people. However, it's a very rare occurrence when someone invents something new in the Real Estate field. After all, it's very straight forward once you cut through the puffery.

I admit that I'm not really sure why this phenomenon exists. I think the authors of these books and courses might be afraid that people won't buy their product if they think that the work might be unoriginal. However collecting, coordinating and disseminating the good information that works from the "not-so-great stuff" that doesn't work which could lose people money is a very important and worthwhile service. Frankly, I think that authors should be straight up and tell people where they learned these things to begin with. I've been studying Real Estate for years. I've become an Expert by putting in the time and effort that's necessary to study, test and apply this information to see what works and what doesn't. Here's what I say about this topic on my website:

> But let me assure you...I did not make this money by knowing "WHAT" to do, or because I'm a genius, or even because I've invented some "Magical World of Disney" system to get money out of Real Estate! To be as blunt and honest as possible, the pure, unadulterated, XXX Rated Truth is that where Real Estate is concerned — there is ABSOLUTELY NOTHING NEW UNDER THE SUN! It's ALL been done before! Regardless of what any 'Guru' says, there's absolutely nothing about Real Estate that hasn't been written about in a book (even mine), or recorded on an audio or video program that can't TELL you WHAT to do!
>
> However knowing WHAT to do and actually DOING IT are two completely different things! Yes! You DO need a system to follow. After all, there are lots of people (myself included) that had to fall on their faces in order to become successful in real estate! But that's because there's got to be an actual Implementation Plan and Action Program that regular people can follow in order to be successful — at Real Estate or anything else!

You see, there's no shame in telling other people where you learned what it is that you're teaching. Let's examine this concept using a field like Science…

Did we **invent** gravity? Or did we **discover** gravity?

Gravity was discovered three centuries ago by a mathematician and physicist named Sir Isaac Newton. He discovered that there is a specific force called gravity that is required to change the speed or direction of something that's moving. This same force he figured must cause apples to fall from trees! After researching this hypothesis he wrote the law of gravity. This law is a mathematical explanation for the way that mass attracts based on his experiments and observations.

Well, that's exactly what a Real Estate course is. You see, I've done literally hundreds of experiments attempting to implement other people's information into my own Real Estate investing business. Sometimes with great success and sometimes experiencing abysmal failure. In any event, through those successes and failures, and by trying to actually implement the ideas of others I ended up making my own observations and eventually put together my own system of doing things using the successful information and methods. So when we talk about the "Real Estate Lifestyle System" or "Jim Canale's System", we mean the collection of information and methods that produced the results I wanted, that were successful, and that made me money. That system is what I teach to others.

So what's a system? Well, when we talk about a business, and Real Estate investing is a business, we're talking about a collection of systems. In most businesses, the systems haven't been invented. Instead, they've been discovered because there is an actual need for the system. For example, in any business you'll find that there are Accounting, Legal, Marketing, Sales, Service/Product Delivery and Customer Service systems. When I start a business, I use an already existing Accounting system and then I tailor it to suit the needs of my business. I don't invent a new Sales system. Instead I find one that works for another business, implement the Sales system and then I modify that system to suit my business needs. So in essence, a business is a collection of systems that you discover and then modify to produce the end result you are looking for…such as a profit! You then can become more sophisticated, successful and profitable in shorter periods of time because you are not reinventing the wheel every time you're getting started.

Simply put, Real Estate investing has been around forever. There really is nothing new under the sun where this subject is concerned. You buy a house, fix up a house and then dispose of the house for a profit—sell it, rent it, whatever. It's the delivery method for that information that makes all the difference in people's ability to learn, use, and make money with the information. Think about it. How many self-help guys are out there? There's Dr. Phil, there's John Grey, there's Wayne Dyer, there's Tony Robbins and many more. You could ask them all about a particular issue and they'd probably be inclined to agree with each others' analysis of the problem. They'd also probably deliver a similar solution to the problem, too. Only their approach to delivering the solution to the problem would vary.

And that's what this book and any other book you can buy on this subject are. A collection of systems and methods that have been discovered by others, and then discovered by me, and then modified or put together in a different order, or tailored for the specific results that I want in my Real Estate investing business.

I want you to do the same thing. Start by following and implementing these systems exactly, and then as you get good at Real Estate investing, start treating these systems as your own, tailoring them to suit your specific needs. Try new things out and seek out new information to add to your arsenal! That's what I've done and now I use these systems to get the results that I want with ease.

Giving Credit Where Credit Is Due

Now for that giving credit part that I talked about earlier. There have been dozens of people's work that I've studied whose information has helped to make me the success story that I've become as a Real Estate Investor. Their discoveries and my modifications to them are interspersed throughout this book and in my Training and Coaching programs. This list is by no means comprehensive, but these are the people's information that I've studied to be able to do what I do. I've separated these people by areas of study. In some cases these experts overlap more than one area, but my goal here is two-fold; first to give them the credit they deserve, and second, to give you a path of experts that are useful to study to expand your Financial Education.

General Business and Economics

Robert Kiyosaki — Author of the *Rich Dad* series of books and programs. Basic accounting principles, reading financial statements, business building and business systems.

Richard Duncan — Author of *The Dollar Crisis* — World economy, valuation of currency and depreciation of the US dollar and its impact on investors.

Daniel Pink — Author of *A Whole New Mind* — Emotional intelligence, decision process, learning techniques and styles.

Chris Anderson — Author of *The Long Tail* — Understanding business cycles.

Laurence Kotlikoff and Scott Burns — Authors of *The Coming Generational Storm* — General economics, Baby Boomer buying cycles and the impact of their coming retirement.

Harry S. Dent — Author of *The Great Bubble Boom* — General economics, Baby Boomer buying cycles and the impact of their upcoming retirement.

Fixing Your Brain—Understanding Wealth Principles

T. Harv Eker — Author of many books and programs (all of which I own) — Concepts and understanding of how people attract and repel money.

Anthony Robbins — Author of many books and programs (all of which I own) — Life, business, time and money strategies.

Dr. John F. Demartini — Author of many books and programs — Life and business transformation strategies.
Gene Landrum — Author of many books — Understanding entrepreneurial behavior patterns.

Dan S. Kennedy — Author of many books and programs — specifically his *Renegade Millionaire System* — Understanding entrepreneurial behavior patterns and belief systems.

Jayne Johnson — Fixes what's stopping you from being successful through a process called Clearing. Jayne's work has been very beneficial to me and I highly recommend meeting her.

Taxation, Accounting and Legal Entities

Diane Kennedy, CPA — Role of taxation in business and use of entities.

Sharon Lechter, CPA — Role of taxation in business and use of entities in Real Estate investing.

C.W. Al Allen — Use of entities for asset protection and tax strategy.

Garret Sutton — Legal structures and entity selection.

Drew Miles — Entities and tax strategies.

Real Estate Specific

Robert Campbell — Real Estate market timing and cycles.

Bill and Cindy Shopoff — Performing due diligence on investment property.

John Burley — Creating Real Estate specific boutique investments.

Ron LeGrand — MAO, ARV, Wholesaling property, Retailing property, Lease options.

John T. Reed — Real Estate investing fundamentals. Note: Regardless of Reed's "Guru" opinions, I own all of his work and it's incredibly smart, accurate, and well thought out — highly recommended reading.

Don Beck — Landlording and Property Management.
Dwan Bent-Twyford and Sharon Restrepo — Wholesaling property.

Robyn Thompson — Rehabbing property and managing Contractors.

Kendra Todd — Managing risk and fear, Real Estate investing fundamentals, sales techniques.

Frank McKinney — Managing risk and fear, Luxury homes, sales techniques.

Ken McElroy — Property Management, due diligence, apartment buildings.

J. Scott Scheel — Apartment buildings and commercial Real-Estate, commercial financing.

David Lindahl — Apartment buildings.

Jimmy Napier — Understanding debt, notes, and creative financing.

Alan Cowgill — Raising capital and private lending.

Keith Cunningham — Raising capital and Negotiation.

Dick Desich — Real Estate investing with your IRA.

Peter Conti and David Finkel — No money down techniques, foreclosure investing .

John W. Schaub — Real Estate investing fundamentals.

Lou Brown — Residential property — buying, selling and lease options. I love his contracts.

Al Lowry — Probate and Foreclosures.

Bill Nickerson — Real estate fundamentals.

All The Rest—Other Important Areas of Study

Napoleon Hill — Masterminding and "Group Think" principles.

R. Buckminster Fuller — Generalized scientific principles and their relationship to business.
Ari Galper — Handling rejection.

Blair Singer — Sales, Team building, performance and accountability.

Bill Brooks — Sales, Team performance and accountability.

Jim Cramer — Stock Market and economic impact.

Warren Buffett — Stock Market, Fundamental and Technical investing, Macroeconomics.

Dan S. Kennedy — Business, Marketing and Sales principles, Copywriting and Time management.

Jay Abraham — Business principles, Marketing strategy

and Copywriting.

Donald Trump — Branding, creative business thinking.

Richard Branson — Branding, creative business thinking.

Robert Ringer — General Sales.

Brian Tracy — Goal Setting and generalized
Success principles.

Yanik Silver — Internet marketing and copywriting.

Michael Gerber — Author of *The E Myth* — Business systems
and NOT staying small.

You will find principles and techniques in this book that come from all of these people, and more! Of course, these experts discovered this information elsewhere, too. For example, Robert Kiyosaki is a student of Buckminster Fuller, Dan Kennedy is a student of Robert Ringer, and Alan Cowgill is a student of Ron LeGrand. We all get our information from somewhere and as you advance in your own Real Estate investing business, you should study their information, too. Don't ever hesitate to study others' work. I even study the work of people that I disagree with! That's how I found out about John Reed's work, and I've profited immensely as a result. After all, how do you get great at anything? Easy! *Commit to Never Stop Learning!*

About the Author

JIM CANALE

America's Real Estate Cashflow Expert

Jim Canale is a Real Estate Investor, an Entrepreneur, an Educator, a Radio Talk Show Host, and now an Author, but that wasn't always the case. Jim started his journey toward financial liberation in the worst possible circumstances. He was living under the Frankford El, the elevated train station at Bridge and Pratt Streets in Philadelphia, as a homeless beggar. Eventually, he made his own way to success and financial freedom by seeking out the top mentors to teach him Real Estate and business skills, and the best coaches to guide him through the ongoing process of making it to the top and staying there!

Jim started his first business when he was just 25 years old. He built computers for small local businesses and sold them for a modest profit. He parlayed that business into a consulting engagement with a Fortune 100 company in Philadelphia for a $10,000-a- month income. Within a year, he turned that engagement into a six-figure salaried position with the top Technology Consulting firm in the United States.

Frustrated and disillusioned with corporate life, Jim started his own Technology Consulting company in 1997. Business was good, but not the 90-to-100 hour work week. Hiring more employees, charging clients more money, trying to replace himself at work, the pressures continued to mount. The time away from his family, and the intense pressures of running a "key-man" business, became too much to take, and he finally threw his hands up in frustration and started seeking out other income-producing avenues.

"That's when I heard about Robert Kiyosaki, and his book Rich Dad Poor, Dad," Jim says. "Robert opened my eyes to a whole different way of looking at making money. One of the key lessons Robert taught me: the Rich don't work for money. Instead, they have their money work for them. And the number one vehicle the Rich use to make money is Real Estate!"

Starting with a 900-square-foot rental home — his first property — less than a decade ago, Jim now owns millions of dollars worth of Real Estate all over Philadelphia, properties which throw off a large amount of passive monthly income. Jim's a big believer anyone can use Real Estate, regardless of market conditions, to leave the corporate Rat Race and start living the lifestyle they've always wanted.

The problem is, Jim says, "When most people consider real estate investing, they think back to those old, late-night infomercials with the gurus in their Hawaiian shirts making empty promises about how people would become millionaires in a only few short months." In Jim's opinion, the idea of "get rich quick" is completely unnecessary. "Most people don't even have a need to become a millionaire," Jim says. "Just a small handful of rental properties, each with just $300 to $400 per month in positive cashflow, could solve almost anybody's financial problems!"

In Jim's own words echoing his new book, **LIVE THE REAL ESTATE LIFESTYLE**...: *"At $300 profit per month, how many simple, little Real Estate deals would you need to never have to make another mortgage payment on your house? What if you never had to pay for your own groceries again? Or cable bill, or electric bill? This is what I mean by Living the Real Estate Lifestyle! That type of freedom and independence is life-changing! I let my Real Estate pay for all the stuff I want and need. I can do it, and you can, too."*

Following in his Mentors' and Coaches' footsteps, Jim Canale is a major proponent of Financial Literacy and Education. He has taught literally thousands of people how to achieve the exact same success he has found in Real Estate and business. You can learn from Jim through his live "experiential" trainings, his free public workshops, his radio programs heard in five major metropolitan cities and suburbs, and now through his own book. His success stories are many, and inspiring. You can join them now at **www.livetherealestatelifestyle.com** to access many more educational tools and programs.

Printed in the United States
203763BV00002B/1-111/P

9 781434 358707